16.²²

Teach Your Dog to Shoplift:
A Tommy Wayne Kramer Collection

by Tom Hine

Teach Your Dog to Shoplift: A Tommy Wayne Kramer Collection
Tom Hine

Self-Published at www.createspace.com

Cover art by Martin Brown
Cover design by Lemon Fresh Design
Interior design by Lemon Fresh Design
www.lemonfreshdesign.com

ISBN: 978-1480146396

Foreword

Tommy Wayne can't stop himself. I can't stop him. I've tried. But not much and not very hard. Tommy Wayne's fans are really rubber-neckers. They can see the carnage coming and they can't look away. They want to giggle but they can only shake their heads and pretend to agree he's just an offensive old hack.

But Tommy Wayne has a gift. You might call it a super power. He can smell a phony a mile away. He can spot the affected, the insincere, the feigned. Oh let him hear "It's for the children," or "We want to give back" and step back.

No one can ignite the outrage of the privileged do-gooder like TWK. Just to hear the bleating of the righteous protectors of 1960s cultural jibberish when Tommy Wayne speaks his mind is a joyful noise to his fans. Dangerous? Only when provoked by another tearful appeal to save a "Grandmother Tree" or an angry demand for a ban on malt liquor from the wine-soaked upper classes.

But Tommy has his soft side too. Mention a great baseball player, or classic game of times past, or a dedicated group of locals rebuilding a ball park, and you have a man as squishy as a worm after a rain.

His wife will tell you that between six packs Tommy does take out the trash, and was housetrained fairly quickly. And he will admit to the sketchy parenting of two remarkably normal children. Otherwise he's a complete crank. But bless him, he's our crank.

K.C. Meadows, Editor
The Ukiah Daily Journal

Dedicated to Teri Capriolo

Oh you are the wind
Beneath my wallet

You are the Disco Ball
That lights up my life

You are my sunscreen
When an ice storm is raging

You are my poem
My trophy, my wife

Also dedicated to Emily Hine & Lucas Hine

If you always suspected something was screwy
about the way you were raised, this should prove it.

Special thanks to

Mike Bradford, Deborah White, Jody Todd, Fred & Joanne Schneiter, Jim Luther, Laura Hamburg, Midge & Frank McMichael, Dave Smith, George Rose, Kip, Phil Baldwin, Kathy Shearn & Rod Coots, Dave & Verle Anderson, Matt Hubley, Kevin Davenport, Sandy Mac Nab, Terry & Melody Mack, Bruce Anderson, Brady Wildberger, Steve Ford, Bonnie Wildberger, Jeff Trouette, Kevin Baldwin & Kitti Houston, Carol Hine, Patricia Littlefield, Laurie Hoenig-Pinches, Torrey Douglass, Jake Stoepler, Brandon Virgin, Jerry DeTreville, Bob Neilson, Jim Matthews, Bill Hine, Dave Poma, Mark Wiget, Tom Allman, Ralph Maize, Peter Page, Mike Haehl, Susan Massini, Gail McAlister, Darca Nicholson, Gene Hoggren, Chris Schallert, Matt Finnegan, Robert Mac Dougall, KC Meadows, Ray Worster, Charity Armstrong, Joe Lee, Ross Egge, Chuck Savage, Mark Pardini, Dan Stacey, Mike & Barbara Mayfield, Ann Moorman, Noah Taxis, Gary Ingle, Captain Mikey, Tom & Anna Daugherty, the MC5, Ray Killion, Bob & Susie Hardie, Greg Sager, Berry Robinson, Tim Kiely, Marge Boynton, Glenn Stelega, Jona Saxby, Kirk Gustafson, Bill Walls, Jim Mayo, Annette Morrison, Steve Mendoza, Darlene Clark-Hine, j. holden, Don & Annie Samson, Mark Hedges, Richard Shoemaker (Berkeley, CA), Richard Shoemaker (Ukiah, CA), Liz & Tom Liberatore, Bob Werra, Ryan Mayfield, Judy Fuente, Cindee Mayfield, Gregg Young, Martin Brown, Mike Rogers, Bruce Poma, Suzanne Haehl, Ron Wilson & Jan Cole-Wilson, Bill Hoover, Willie Gordon, Bill Mac Nab, Mike Geniella, Emma & Jimmy Eldridge, Ross Liberty,

and, more than anyone, Peter Hine.

Contents

Contents, continued

Assignment: Ukiah

Ukiah is a weird, boring and ugly place filled with people from somewhere else who couldn't make it there, plus all the locals who haven't yet figured out how to leave.

It's an odd and surreal town. People constantly tell each other how fortunate they are to live in such a paradise, such a Shangri La populated by gentle visionaries congregating in a lovely oasis here in beautiful Northern California. These folks see a vibrant small town filled with charming and fascinating people. They also see auras and chakras and soul mates. They visit yoga studios and they shop at the Farmer's Market. They believe the spirits of the Native Americans infuse the tapestry of modern day life in Ukiah, filling the valley with a dreamlike ambience. Maybe they believe Priuses fly.

The reality is that Ukiah is a town full of tire shops and mattress outlets and closed storefronts with graffiti scrawled on the plywood covering broken windows. Losers wander the streets with their dogs and their backpacks, having come to Ukiah to get in on the illicit drug trade that keeps the local economy afloat.

It's a dry, bleak, sun-choked valley eight months of the year. Greenery suffocates while weeds flourish in vacant lots full of dust, thistle, a few dead tires and some Taco Bell wrappers. Newspaper sheets are blown flat up against chainlink fences. In the winter it rains. It's always depressing and sometimes it floods.

Old homes and charming buildings have been systematically torn down and burned down over the decades, replaced with one-story, corrugated metal storage shops and Kwikeemarts run by people from Pakistan.

Ukiah is a town without a heart, without a soul, without a decent bar with a good jukebox. This is where outlaw bikers and meth cookers mate with welfare queens to produce a shiftless, listless underclass of those inclined toward criminality, and are good at it. They're on the bottom rung.

At the top is a layer of smug, college educated, politically correct professionals who make fine wages and live on the fashionable west side of town. They drive expensive imported cars with "Question Authority" bumperstickers and spend their days pretending to minister to the needs of the underclass. But criminals and welfare recipients don't much listen to the case managers and welfare workers and therapists even when judges and probation officers tell them to. The underclass has its own way of questioning the authorities.

And waiting on the sidelines are the children. Many are teens, all are bored. It's always mildly surprising more youngsters don't commit suicide around here.

If you were forced to put together a list of Ukiah's 10 best restaurants you'd have to put Denny's no lower than third or fourth. The Water Trough bar might make the list with a menu of draft beer, beef jerky and 50-cent bags of pretzels. Walmart is the most popular store in town. Nothing is in second place.

The downtown area is a forlorn few blocks trying desperately to look perky, just like those towns where tourists visit and have fun. But tourists don't visit Ukiah and never will. The town has been on a decades-long quest to increase tourism and has not yet gained an inch. It's because tourism officials don't see that Ukiah is a tacky, ugly blotch rather than a magical mystical land of gifted artists.

Slogans and banners promising Wine and Cheese and Art and Community and Dance can't camouflage the gnarly nightmare of a drive from one end of Ukiah to the other, a six-mile stretch of relentless visual atrocities unequaled by any city I've ever seen, and I've seen Orlando and Fresno and Modesto. And that six-mile stretch is a drive that every would-be tourist has made, though probably not twice.

Every year more money gets spent on groups and agencies promising to deliver the long-awaited tour buses and the endless stream of vacationers that never materialize. Don't worry, they say. Next year more funding will be directed to new billboards and bigger brochures. We're in the process of coming up with some new slogans. That should do the trick.

The once grand Palace Hotel has been closed 30 years and is rotting away right in the center of town. The lovely old post office has been closed, its operations moved to a warehouse out near the freeway. The courthouse, after some hundred years' use, will be replaced by a new bright and shiny model either a few blocks or a few miles away. It will be ugly. It will look like a motel. What's remaining of downtown will simply fold up, a heap of ugly buildings collapsed upon each other. City officials do nothing about any of this because city officials have not yet been notified it is happening,

"Leaders" instead focus on banning plastic bags and certain brands of coffee shops; they invest in alternative technologies like wind and flying carpets. Council members chirpily remind the citizens that the future looks great. Our homeless population has increased for the seventeenth straight year, and those tour buses should be arriving in the spring!

Welcome to Ukiah. Jump right in, the water's fine.

Ukiah's good old days, and how I ruined them

I first came to Ukiah long, long ago—when pterodactyls wheeled against a crimson sky, teepee burners dotted the landscape and the highway to Hopland was just two lanes wide.

And no matter how much has changed since my earliest days here, many things are exactly the same. Ukiah is still the ugliest town in California and in danger of being the ugliest in all the land. It remains a ghastly strip with more yoga centers and tattoo parlors than cool bars and decent radio stations.

And the road to Hopland is still two lanes wide, even though traffic on Highway 101 doubles every decade.

So I first arrived in Ukiah back in the 1970s. There I was at the Ben Hur gas station at the north end of town with my long stringy hair and flies buzzing around my head. I wasn't hung up on hygiene, man. I had my VW bus and I had my old lady. I also had a fully functioning olfactory system, and when I took a deep breath of the Masonite-enriched local air, and then took another hard squint down State Street I quickly moved to Cloverdale. Total time spent in Ukiah on my first-ever visit: Seven minutes.

And what brought me back to Ukiah? One mistake after another.

In the beginning there were unemployment benefits and other government cheese. It was certainly not all hardship and misery, not with a sizeable crop of hippie chicks to amuse me and marijuana selling at very reasonable rates; most dealers would take food stamps or cash.

Plus the weather was pretty good compared to Cleveland. So Ukiah indeed had some positives but the problem was that other people began noticing, and they started moving here too.

And Ukiah started changing.

It wasn't much at first. No reason for alarm. A natural foods restaurant opened on Main Street. There was something called Pegasus Books where the collected works of Ram Dass and Richard Brautigan could be browsed or shoplifted.

Next, an alternative newspaper. And yurts. Then there was Greenfield Ranch, home to communal living, organic farmers, and serial murderers. Ukiah would have been better off with a toxic waste site out there on Orr Springs Road, but at the time Greenfield seemed like, cool and far-out. And it certainly was.

Then before you could say "Class K Housing" there were shops selling beads and crystals and roach clips and rolling papers, plus bongs and incense and brown sand candles and tie-dye t-shirts.

School buses arrived filled with various astrologers, poets, dulcimer players and tarot specialists. Also on board: thieves, druggies, parolees, sex predators and various scam artists.

I'm not sure when the tipping point took place, but when it did Old Ukiah didn't put up much of a struggle. Aside from a few "America Love It or Leave It" bumper stickers and the occasional clear-thinking letter to the editor, there was no real resistance to the mob of ill-bred, semi-civilized, impolite invaders.

Most of the newcomers were college graduates who had utter contempt for millworkers and truck drivers and housewives. They were well-trained in confrontational politics and quickly got down to business once they had established themselves in the area.

Meetings were crowded with outraged back-to-the-landers demanding the right to live in plumbing-free shanties without electricity that would have been deemed inadequate by the middle of the 19th century. They then set about raising their children in a sugar-free, protein-free, vaccine-free, TV-free, knowledge-free, bathing-free existence.

They started "schools" where "teachers" carefully avoided imparting anything worth learning to the kids, and instead emphasized caring and sharing and recycling and self-esteem.

Dear friends, if I'd known how this was all going to turn out I'd have called the police and had everyone arrested, including me. But I probably didn't have a dime for a phone call, and besides, the phone company was known as Ma Bell back then and was a huge enemy of planet hippie. I never knew why.

The oldtimers, being naturally polite and friendly and generous and tolerant, tried their best to accommodate the newcomers and make them feel welcome. The swarm responded by elbowing the farmers and ranchers and loggers out of the way, then selling off their land in 20-acre parcels that all became hemp production facilities.

And that, children, is how Compassionate Cannabis Dispensaries came to be!

"Look at me everybody!"

There are plenty of candidates for Biggest Jerk in the World awards. Perhaps you'll find a favorite among the following:

- Oil company executives
- Methamphetamine cookers
- Social workers
- NBA players
- Used car salesmen
- Deepak Chopra
- Fitness instructors

All are worthy of consideration as objects of our scorn, but I have a group that towers above all others in terms of narcissism, arrogance and uselessness. I speak, of course, of bicyclists.

No, I don't mean you and your 8-year old tootling around Todd Grove Park, dad on the ancient Schwinn Cruiser, daughter on the used pink Barbie Doll bike with training wheels. No, I mean *bicyclists*.

I mean the dipwads who squeeze into yellow-and-black polyester outfits, strap on their vented ultra-high tech wind resistant DorkMaster helmets, mount their $12,000 titanium two wheel machines and take to the road exactly one-half block ahead of you as you drive to work. It's those smug, sneering, pedaling creeps riding their hotshot bicycles I'm talking about.

Who do they think they are, other than the most precious people in the galaxy? Bicyclists obviously love themselves, and why shouldn't they? Behold their skintight orange-pink-purple-and-silver lycra outfits! Gaze upon them in rapt admiration as they pedal O So Furiously down a long hill while they closely observe their perfect pumping thighs and their sleek, taut forearms. *Adonis lives within me!* they whisper to themselves.

Meanwhile you, a carbonload dinosaur in your old Plymouth van, trail along behind the pack of clown-suited sillies and wonder to yourself why they can't at least move over so you can get to work. As in "Share The Road" which is a bumpersticker that every one of these rolling bicycle pukes has glued to his Toyota Prius.

Of course the bike brigade doesn't care if you get to work on time, because they understand that everyone's real job is to save the planet.

But here's my question to the fabulous marvels who ride bicycles in packs and look like Kodachrome insects as they block traffic here and there and all around town: What is it with the dressing up?

Why is it you bunch of showoffs have to dress up like Lance Armstrong in order to ride your bikes around Ukiah? Do you guys dress up like Dale Earnhart when you drive your car to Safeway?

When you have plane tickets to fly from SFO to JFK do you show up at the airport dressed like Charles Lindberg or Eddie Rickenbacker—you know, leather bomber jacket, goggles, long white scarf and a flight map?

If a neighborhood pal invites you to a backyard poolside barbecue do you arrive outfitted in an official Jacques Cousteau Aqua 5000 model deep sea wetsuit, complete with US Navy-issue breathing tanks guaranteed to work at 7500 feet below sea level?

Well then why in the world do you need to look like Greg Lemond when wheeling a bicycle out of a garage on a Thursday afternoon in order to ride six blocks to the post office?

Adult bicyclists are immature goofs playing dress-up and make-believe. They are the most selfish people you are likely to encounter in your everyday life as they roll herd-like up and down the hills of the Boonville Road, staying three abreast to prevent cars from slipping by, and swerving quickly across lanes in case one tries.

These are the people I want rounded up and sent to Guantanamo Bay.

Next time you encounter a batch of bicyclists cluttered around a coffee shop with their bicycles and their garish costumes completely blocking the sidewalk, punch one of them right in the nose.

But first make sure you're wearing a pair of official Sonny Liston model Everlast boxing trunks.

Awards of Dubious Distinction

Mendocino County
Employee of the Month

Coolest Tattoo, Fourth Grade
Division, Frank Zeek Elementary

Nicest House in Calpella

Time to reinvent the Peace Corps

Let's remake the Peace Corps so it's relevant and useful to local needy people.

What better location than Mendocino County to bring together folks who want to make the world a better place? Our area is filled with people who think the 1960s was the greatest era in history, and that the Peace Corps best exemplified those times. Let's unleash their energy and build a bold new future! Let's give their idealism a chance to show the world what people committed to hope and change can do.

SIGN UP FOR TWO YEARS AT PLOWSHARES

What an opportunity! You'll be able to freely mingle with the underprivileged when you bring food from your home to Plowshares and prepare the day's lunch. You'll serve hungry folks who've stopped by for a free meal on their way to get food stamp cards.

Next you'll clear the tables and clean the dining area, then wash dishes and put things away before getting started on dinner, which has to be ready in 45 minutes.

Your efforts mean Plowshare diners never have to do demeaning work like mopping and scrubbing, which is slave labor, frankly. Such toiling is harmful to their self-esteem. You'll be helping create a more harmonious world without class divisions.

BRING THE GIFT OF LOVE TO LOCAL GANG MEMBERS

Starting now you can Be the Change you've dreamed about. You and your spouse will live on Laws Avenue and infiltrate local gangs, one of you as a Norteno, the other as a Sureno. Once embedded, you'll teach alternatives to violence and utilize art therapy techniques to achieve peaceful conflict resolution.

Living among these exotic people you'll participate in their colorful lifestyles and help preserve their customs and rituals, such as the nighttime spray paint application of indigenous hieroglyphics on local buildings.

You'll even receive a free gang tattoo as part of your initiation, although you should remember to request yours be done in henna, rather than in a fellow-gang member's blood.

Also, when you get arrested and sent to prison, you and your spouse will have earned valuable gang experience so you'll be readily accepted into the Aryan Brotherhood.

Let prison reform begin with you!

STUPID FARMERS NEED YOUR HELP

Our slow-witted but harmless local ranchers have been hard hit by economic downturns in cow and sheep crops. Modest and uncomplaining, most farmer-types are unlikely to ask for help. But that doesn't mean you can't invite yourself into their lives for their own good.

First you'll homestead on their property and wait for these shy, simple people to eventually make contact. Next, instruct them on sustainable hemp production along with dry irrigation techniques that you once read about in a copy of "Heal the Earth Now!" magazine. Demand that they build and use a compost toilet and you will have changed not just their attitudes, but their lives.

You can also help them update their dreary wardrobes. Denim work shirts with Ben Davis trouser pairings are *so Arkansas!*

END THE CYCLE OF POVERTY ALL BY YOURSELF

You'll live and teach simultaneously when you move in with an impoverished family headed by a heroic single mother. Her eight children (by eleven different men) will benefit from your constant reminders that their helplessness is a result of the harsh, greedy, exploitive capitalist system that forces them to go twice yearly to the Social Services Department to learn about all the new benefits they can sign up for.

As a member of their community you'll learn their quaint customs: neighborhood squabbles, calling 9-1-1 to ask what channel American Idol is on, and filling shopping carts with Ding-Dongs, Kool Whip, Pop Tarts and diet cola in three-gallon jugs. Remember that in this unique culture it's dinnertime whenever you're near the kitchen.

INTERVENING IN NEGLECTED LIVES

Trapped in remote locations like Covelo and Potter Valley, many marijuana growers are without access to vital services such as job placement agencies, law enforcement, and income tax preparation assistance. You can be the bridge.

This population, living in the shadows of society, will benefit immensely when you distribute free pamphlets inviting them to explore career options at Walmart, and to help them establish Neighborhood Watch programs with the help of a friendly Sheriff's Department Community Services Officer.

When you move into a so-called "commune" of marijuana growers you'll quickly learn (in a non-judgmental way, of course) about their lifestyles. Diverting stream waters for ag use, for example, is an ancient tradition dating back 20 years or more. Their barter economy means you'll learn firsthand about retail pot distribution and meth production techniques. (*Note: For this Peace Corps assignment you must be willing to ingest cocaine and spend winters in Hawaii or the Bahamas.*)

The time for a Peace Corps 2.0 is now and we (well, you) are the people to do it. Me, I'll be down at Plowshares having lunch.

Free cigarettes for all teenagers!

Smoking is a pleasure enjoyed in every society that has access to tobacco, and if I could give one tiny bit of advice to all my young readers it would be that I think you should smoke cigarettes.

Being young is cool and smoking is cool, and the people who tell you otherwise are pious old social workers who get paid to tell other people how to live.

The boring phonies who will scold you about smoking are all ex-hippie diploads, and if you start smoking the first benefit you'll reap is not having to hang out with people like them. Their idea of a whole lotta fun is a second-helping of low-fat granola before heading off to that yoga class at the college. Then it's back home to listen to a nice soothing "Music of the Incas" CD before going to bed. At 8:30. On a Saturday.

But your friends won't be like that. Your friends will smoke. They will smoke and drink and party and go to Paris and smoke a bunch while wearing berets and drinking cheap wine and smoking some more. Then you'll come home with a lot of great new friends and by then you'll be an excellent smoker.

Meanwhile, the hippie dude social worker will have eaten 900 buckets of yogurt, consumed a million gallons of bottled Evian water, and not smoked a single cigarette. Who would you rather be?

Now, there are certainly some drawbacks to smoking and I want you to be ready. First, you'll get an avalanche of complaints from all the boring non-smokers. Since these are the same people who are always whining and sniveling about something, it would be nice of you to have them direct their anger at you for a while. It'll save the rest of us having to listen to them cry and sputter about Big Oil and Sarah Palin and the sad plight of endangered mosquitoes.

You'll also have to listen to dreary sermons from these same dweebs about how very very bad it is to smoke, and they will tell you many big lies to make you believe it. They always start with one about how 17 billion people die every day from smoking.

This is obvious nonsense. Are they saying that if those 17 billion people just didn't smoke they'd live forever? Well, that's the point: everybody dies, whether they smoke or not. But the anti-smoking zealots want you to believe that in our smoke-free future no one will ever die, or even cough, I guess.

It's the same absurd reasoning they use when they tell you smoking is what increases health care costs. But if smokers are all hurrying up and dying, how does that increase healthcare costs? If they're dead how can they run up a big bill at Ukiah Valley Medical Center?

The truth is that it's the healthiest people—the people who live to be 104 by being hooked up to tubes and masks and machines—that cost so much. If those selfish old fogies would get out of the way health care costs would drop a bunch.

So instead of complaining about smokers, it's the health-nut crowd we ought to be going after. It's organic carrots and wheat germ that ought to be taxed, not cigars and Skoal and Marlboros.

People who are vegetarians and spend all day at the health club are the selfish pigs who will live an extra 30 years (the last 25 years hooked up to expensive medical equipment that hasn't even been invented yet). There's your drain on health care costs right there.

Smokers do the socially responsible thing and die young. A smoker might only make it to 80, thus saving the world a bundle in medical costs, but will have a grand time of it, smoking and drinking and enjoying a life well lived.

Cigarettes make the good times better, and the bad times less stressful. They make sexy women sexier. In a cocktail lounge a cigarette is as harmonious as a saxophone in a jazz quartet.

But school teachers and social workers and other professional "helpers" won't let you hear of it. They pretend they care about your health but they don't. They care about their jobs, and a big part of their jobs is to lecture kids about smoking.

They think it's a good deal for you to not smoke and for you to spend your final five years on earth unconscious while strapped to a hospital bed. The alternative? A life with at least a bit of risk, a little adventure, some friends who have fun and aren't all pasty and afraid.

Now to get started you're going to need some cigarettes, the price of which keeps going up because politicians and social workers and teachers want more money to fund their stupid programs to tell kids not to smoke. So cigarettes aren't cheap.

But still, you can buy them for less than 25 cents each, and you've been spending that much on candy bars all your life. If you and your friends just cut back on what you spend on your school lunches every day you'll have plenty of money for a carton of Camels,

Start smoking tomorrow, and you and your friends can begin dreaming about how cool you'll all be, wearing berets and smoking in Paris.

One beer short

A long time ago I found myself up in Covelo working with a friend named Joe Lee. We were talking with uncooperative people about irrelevant events with negligible results.

We spent the day in a seething, beastly Covelo heat not many people have experienced, and certainly not twice. It might have been 140 degrees. Felt like Centigrade. By 4 p.m. our tongues were thickening and our vision was a series of black dots and wavy lines. The "work" was done and so we pointed Joe's Ford Bronco toward Ukiah. It was so hot.

We stopped at Dan's Market to get provisions for the ride home, which means we went straight to the beer cooler. Joe pulled a couple of nice frosty cans of Foster's Lager off the chrome shelf, and I stood staring at the glass door. "What'll ya have, li'l buddy?" he asked, waving a twenty. "I'm buying." I stared glumly at all those happy quarts and forties and six packs, and quietly said "Nothing."

Joe's face melted to innocent puppy dog bewilderment. I sighed and explained how my new boss would take special delight in firing me if he had the merest suspicion I'd been drinking on the job. "B-b-but we're in Covelo, and it's July!" Joe sputtered, as if that was sufficient reason to suspend petty work-related rules and regulations.

We left the store and headed south on Highway 162. In about a mile we turned right on Poonkinney Road. I'd been beerless the entire mile. Joe handed me a stick of beef jerky but it had no meaning. I gazed out the smeared window of the Bronco and gasped for air. Actually I gasped for air conditioning, but Joe said he'd disconnected it. "Gets better mileage that way, li'l buddy" he said cheerfully. I sat wondering what radiator fluid tasted like.

The miles dragged by and so did the scraggly brush lining the dirt road. I looked up and saw a team of vultures wheeling overhead like an apparition against a white-baked sky. I saw cactus and the bleached bones of dead cattle lying 'neath a pitiless sun. Man it was hot.

We spent most of July bucking and rocking and eating dust on our way to Dos Rios. And what is Dos Rios, you ask? Well, Dos Rios is where all the heat in California gets together for meetings. Suck on a blow torch, set fire to your toes, plunge your face into boiling water and welcome to Dos Rios!

We pulled over and stepped out of the truck and into a dusty turnout. The air didn't stir except to rub its molecules against each other to generate more heat. Trees cast no shadows. I could feel beads of sweat dripping off my pancreas.

Joe leaned against the grille of his truck. He tipped the over-sized can of Foster's to his lips and took in a series of four-ounce doses of ice cold medicine. Foamy beer flecked his mustache. He began to softly hum and I leaned closer. It was Beethoven's "Ode to Joy." I hated him.

Dear reader, this all took place 18 or so years ago and although it makes no sense, I have continued to believe that Joe Lee, in some peculiar cosmic sense, hidden in a fundamental kernel of eternal justice, still owes me a beer. I've even told him so.

And Joe agrees! He has conceded many times during the past decade that there is indeed a debt in Tommy's life ledger, and that I am owed a beer. A big beer, I remind him. He always nods somberly. He knows. He understands that unless things are made right I will go to my grave one beer short.

*   *   *

I sometimes see Joe Lee in my dreams and the dream is always the same: I am standing on the street not far from my house, and am peering off into the distance where the road curves out of sight. And then, from a long way off I can see a glowing chariot coming toward me out of the sky.

Joe Lee is holding the reins of six horses—are those Clydesdales?!?—and he's smiling a big smile. He's leaning from the chariot as it floats my way. The wind is in his hair and he's holding a huge mug that must have five gallons of beer in it. And then it's all like in slow motion and his arm sweeps by in a long smooth arc and he hands that frosty mug to me and then he's soaring toward the clouds high above the trees along the horizon and he's shouting "Guess that makes us even now, huh li'l buddy?"

Well yeah, Joe. But only in my dreams.

Awards of Dubious Distinction (Cont'd)

First Place, annual Sidewalk
Chalk Art competition

Best dog at pound

Driving me crazy

Your neighbor is out of town but his wife isn't so the two of you hop in the car and head to the Mendocino Coast for a scandalous weekend. Up you go to Willits, roll west out on Highway 20, and here's my question:

What is the absolute worst vehicle you could be stuck behind on the 33-mile journey from Willits to Fort Bragg?

(A) Logging truck
(B) Greyhound bus
(C) Great big recreational vehicle full of vacationers from Cleveland gawking at redwood trees and spotted owls
(D) Toyota Prius with a "Coexist" bumper sticker

No veteran Ukiahan has to think very long to come up with the right answer on this one. Nothing goes slower than a Prius in single lane traffic, especially if the driver knows there are dozens of impatient drivers piling up behind.

Why? Because people who drive a Prius know how other people should live their lives. Prius drivers know what you should eat, how much yoga you should do, for whom you should vote and which therapist might be a good fit. People with this kind of wisdom have no problem telling you how fast to drive.

Prius owners are the smartest, most conscientious and virtuous people on Earth. They are saving the planet, for Goddess sake, and if they are smart enough to protect us all from planetary annihilation then they are smart enough to know how fast you should drive to Fort Bragg.

A Prius owner (or are they Prius guardians?) understands that a drive on Highway 20 is a sacred journey through the magical redwood forests, and is not something to hurry. It is to be savored in a serene and tranquil fashion.

You are to live each moment as it unfolds and touches your loving heart. You are to go placidly amidst the haste. You are to ignore the ambulance sirens and the bakery trucks honking their horns. Prius drivers have naught but disdain for the grubby world of paramedics and commerce and feel no compelling reason to be put upon by them in their rush to pass by.

How dare they interrupt the calm and glowing inner peace the Prius Man has achieved? "Turnout?" says Prius Man. "What turnout?" And he goes back to listening to Spencer Brewer on KZYX as the miles slowly unspool 'neath his teeny tiny carbon footprint.

Why are Prius owners so smug and pleased with themselves? Because to drive a Prius is a wondrous act, a choice so filled with generosity and with so fervent a commitment to the future that common folks should acknowledge their moral superiority. Peasants (truck drivers, for instance) should understand that at the wheel of every Prius is an eco-warrior.

Prius drivers care. They make a statement. They make a difference. They make me laugh.

As for that trip to the coast we're not even to Irmulco Road yet and already Misty and I have gone through the 12-pack that was supposed to last until we got to the motel. If we don't turn back now we'll die of parched throats before the stupid Prius up ahead ever lets us by.

And if we get stuck behind another Prius on the way back to Ukiah, Misty's husband will be there before we are.

A Christmas to remember

I'll always remember the Christmas of 1993. We were working our way through the holiday gifts—there was discarded wrapping paper piled knee deep around the living room—and my kids were experiencing the numb, semi-comatose incomprehension of all the love Santa had shoveled upon them.

I had opened a few gifts: a coffee mug, a necktie, a book about Rocky Colavito, and then I picked up a clumsily wrapped present from my brother in New York. I tore it open and fished out a small bag. Inside the bag was . . . a Rolex.

My brother had sent me a Rolex wristwatch for Christmas.

I blinked but I don't think I breathed. I gazed down at my new Rolex Perpetual Oyster wristwatch and blinked again. I couldn't have been more surprised if Peter had parked a Cadillac Brougham convertible in my driveway, or stuffed my stocking with Cyndi Lauper.

I hefted my new watch in my right hand and I felt a bit dizzy. A Rolex is the last word in luxury timepieces and as I cradled it in my hand I understood why. The shimmering gold and silver gleamed and glowed like treasure meant for King Tut. The thick, heavy bracelet had substance and gravity and a quiet beautiful dignity.

I slipped it onto my left wrist and locked the silver clasp. It felt like an accomplishment. It felt like a hard-earned trophy, like an Olympic medal. It felt warm and rich. I felt unworthy.

I also felt cheap. I'd bought brother Pete a $50 sweater from MacNab's that year, and although that's a terrific gift any old holiday season it seemed meager in comparison. This had suddenly been transformed into the Christmas of a Lifetime. I went to the phone and called him.

True to form he downplayed the enormity of his present to me. He agreed it was a gift of immense value but insisted I deserved it, and that the watch's cost, given the length and depth of our relationship, was ultimately modest.

Our family ties will stretch out into the misty future, he said, and predicted I'd still be wearing the watch half a century later. I would then bestow it on my son, said Pete, and after that the Rolex would disappear into the hands of distant and unborn generations, with the cost ultimately dissolving into nickels a year. He was proud to have purchased it for me. And then, in the spirit of the season, he generously pointed out how much he appreciated a top quality Pendleton sweater in the face of another cold New York winter.

Next I called my sister, and after the initial holiday greetings it bubbled out that Pete had sent me a Rolex. There was a short pause and Carol changed the subject. Jealous, I wondered? Oh well, maybe next year he'd send her to Bali for the holidays.

I spent the remainder of Christmas in a light, happy trance, always and forever aware of the weighty badge of opulence that caressed my left wrist. At that point I wouldn't have traded my Rolex for the Cadillac AND Cyndi Lauper.

My sister's birthday is December 26 and I called to wish her a happy one. It was during that call I noticed the small date window on the watch face still read "25." It hadn't rolled over to show the next day. I started to say something about the Rolex and Carol interrupted me to talk about the weather in Pennsylvania.

Oddly enough I had to call my sister a third straight day in order to ask her about exchanging a gift she'd sent my daughter. At some point I mentioned to Carol that I was feeling pretty embarrassed about getting a Rolex from Pete and only giving him a sweater.

There was a long pause on the other end of the line. Finally, through gritted teeth, I could hear my sister exhale.

"Tommy," she said in a flat, level tone, "He bought. That watch. On. The. Street. For about 20 dollars. It's. Not. A. Rolex. *Are you stupid?!?*"

I thought: My brother gave me a fake Rolex??

I quickly thought again: My brother gave me a fake Rolex!!

In a billionth of a second it all clicked in place. The Rolex had been in a *bag*, for God's sake! It didn't keep the right time! And to top it all off, Pete had been lording it over me for the past three days, portraying himself as some wise and benevolent philanthropist. I'd been had, no doubt about it.

He'd given me a twenty dollar watch for Christmas, the chintzy trickster! That's less than half what I paid for the sweater! I'd been swindled! I'd been screwed! Darn right it's just nickels a year!! I took the cheap crummy watch off and stuck it in my sock drawer.

A few years later my 11-year old needed a watch so I dug it out and tossed it to him. Surprisingly, it was running and it showed the correct time. That was in 2001.

To this day the Faulex runs perfect. It hangs off my kid's arm like a horseshoe around a toothpick, but he's smart enough not to give away its cheap secret. His friends gawk. Worth every penny of that twenty bucks.

Mixing drinks out of your medicine cabinet

We all find ourselves occasionally marooned where there are no alcoholic beverages to drink. We may be in a dry county or perhaps in a household where alcohol is forbidden because of either religious or AA reasons.

But you, the drinker, need not panic. Instead, take careful inventory of what is available, then roll up your sleeves and get to work. Examples?

SCENARIO I

You are visiting your mother-in-law at Christmastime. Your wife has made it clear—by removing the bottle of Captain Morgan Spiced Rum from your suitcase—there will be no repeat of last year's catastrophic drunken holiday.

But remember: every pantry and spice rack in America has vanilla extract, and if you read the label you'll see it contains 40% alcohol. You're set for tonight. But you're going to need an early-morning eye-opener, and with the nearest bar (and Bloody Mary) 75 miles away, I suggest you try one of these:

Nyquila Sunrise

2 oz Nyquil cherry-flavored cough syrup
2 oz Scope mouthwash
2 Alka Seltzer tablets

While others are having ham and eggs for breakfast, assemble above ingredients from the medicine cabinet.

Thoroughly rinse drinking glass your mother-in-law keeps her dentures in. Crush Alka Seltzer tablets on sink top using edge of glass. Wet rim of glass, coat with crushed powder.

Pour mouthwash into glass, then slowly add Nyquil. Do not stir.

Admire the subtle colors, piquant bouquet and the thrilling effervescent zest. Contrast the sharp metallic tang of mouthwash to the effulgent warmth of cough syrup.

Here's to fresh breath!

SCENARIO II

You work for Mendocino County and understand there's a strict No Alcohol policy. But you also need to impress Jennifer, the newly hired Administrative Assistant in your department, so you suggest a 4:15 p.m. rendezvous in the copy room.

In the meantime go to Rite Aid and get ingredients for a

Listertini

4 oz Listerine
¼ oz Oragel (baby gum anesthetic)
Dash of Witch Hazel

Chill above in office fridge. Stem glasses are a dead giveaway, so serve in a pair of those "You Don't Have to be Crazy to Work Here But it Helps" coffee mugs. In lieu of olives, drop in two Ricola cherry cough drops.

Ballpoint pens make excellent swizzle sticks; clink cups with Jennifer. Enjoy while discussing whether Warner-Lambert or Proctor & Gamble had the better vintage in 2011.

SCENARIO III

It's time to go see grandma at the Final Days nursing home over there on South Dora. It would sure be a lot easier to visit if there was an Open Bar at the weekly bingo games. But when granny and her roommate are sleeping go through their medications and mix up a big batch of

Geritoladas

One bottle Geritol
One bottle Paregoric anti-diarrheal medicine
One bottle liquid Iron supplement
Four time-release dermal morphine patches

Mix liquid ingredients in any one of the numerous empty FTD flower vases lying about. Twist morphine patches repeatedly, then tear apart and drop small pieces into liquid.

Allow mixture to steep 15 minutes; decant and toast yourself for having concocted a beverage that is its own remedy for the hangover it will soon bring you.

Offer leftover Geritoladas to the best-looking nurse. If she's actually willing to try one ask for her phone number. She sounds like she might be fun.

(Send $1 for the "TWK Guide for Mixing Drinks When There's No Liquor Store." Recipes include The Cosmopolident, Benadryl Alexander, Cepacol Sling and Dristopolitan.)

All dogs go to Heaven

We sent Snuppy up to the big dog park in the sky last week and by now I suppose she's queen of the whole place. And why not? She was, after all, the world's greatest dog.

Isn't it strange that so many people have the world's greatest dog? And despite the statistical improbability of so many dogs all being the best, I cheerfully accept that it is true. I have known several myself.

Ours came into the house as Carmen Capriolo, but as things in the pet universe often go, she became Snuppy the Dog. She stayed with us more than 14 years, then departed after having fulfilled her royal duties to instruct us on living a life more meaningful, a life more filled with grace, a life that celebrates the Doggess in us all.

I think if you were to live your life more like Snuppy lived hers you would be a happier person. You would never lose sleep over stock market fluctuations, for instance, nor would the cost of gasoline trouble you. If you met Nancy Pelosi you'd no doubt like her just fine.

You would not get upset if you heard your eldest pup was seeing a Dalmatian. And you would never feel greedy except twice a day when the crunchies were getting poured into your bowl and the cat was loitering nearby.

But Snuppy wasn't just wise and gracious. She also had inner beauty, was fiercely devoted and completely loyal. Frankly though, her breath wasn't all that great.

Did someone say Beauty? Snuppy had no flash, no glitz, no makeup, not even a diamond-studded collar. Just a cheery, jaunty, circus dog prance and that patented Golden Retriever smile, plus snow white feathers against her gleaming gold coat.

Disposition? If you had Snuppy's ever-loving personality you would never again think of whacking your spouse with a meat cleaver. Instead, you would do what Snuppy would do: use the cleaver to chop sirloin steak to mix in with the crunchies for a superb candlelit dinner for you and your mate. Unless your mate is a cat.

Everyone loved Snuppy and Snuppy loved everyone. She especially loved kids. Especially toddler kids carrying food approximately 22 inches off the ground.

And she loved to run and walk and strike terror, as best she could, into the hearts of neighborhood squirrels from the strained end of a five-foot leash. And she loved to sleep, either in front of the door or in front of the fire or on the old leather chair that will smell funky forever because of all the sleeping she did on it.

Most of all she loved the woman she thought was her mother but who was actually my wife. Snuppy loved Teri in ways that surpass understanding. We could all learn.

She was rewarded for her wonderfulness by living a long and happy life. She had a big yard full of intriguing things, including cats and squirrels, and she had a young boy she'd taught to play fetch with a tennis ball. Her crunchies were served daily at 8 a.m. and 5 p.m. sharp.

But Snuppy grew old. She slowed down on her walks, then shortened them as the years wore her out. Next she quit walking altogether. There were times she grew indifferent to her crunchies, which would be like you growing indifferent to oxygen. The good side: as she got old and frail and wobbly she got to visit her very best friends (other than Emily and Lucas) who happened to be Dr. Ed Haynes and his assistant, Todd, at the Ukiah Veterinary Hospital. Snuppy loved to go to the vet.

But in the end that wasn't enough.

Someone may have seen Snuppy in the final months and told you she had grown old and was no longer the beautiful dog she had once been.

That person would be wrong. Never was Snuppy lovelier than in her last days. Although she was blind and deaf to anything less than an airplane falling through the roof, she never lost her poise. She walked with a limp that made me wince, but there was a quiet dignity in her slow, halting steps.

She lost weight yet retained a sleek, serene demeanor befitting her grande dame status. But old age kept up its relentless attack. Snuppy spent her final weeks, hours and minutes lying on the cool tile of her home's entryway.

Gone was her spark and her spirit and her endless joy, replaced by a calm tranquility that also seemed endless. I hope it is.

Life's Simple Pleasures

The satisfying *crunch* of a snail crushed
underfoot on the garden pathway

The roaring racetrack sounds from the Ukiah
Speedway on a summer weekend evening.

And a bag of chips to go

It was back in the 1970s when a bunch of my hippie friends and I, being otherwise unemployable, started a group home in Redwood Valley. In addition to giving us a source of income, a group home provided counties an option to place their juvenile delinquents somewhere other than a landfill.

You probably think group home work is a bunch of counseling and therapy and woo woo voodoo goo. But mostly it's getting kids to school on time and trying to minimize their contact with law enforcement.

Another thing about working in a group home is that you're always driving kids somewhere and then later driving them back.

So there I was on a summer afternoon hauling a bunch of guys back from one Bay Area event or another, and amid the usual teenage banter and chatter—which could be surprisingly amusing, by the way—came a voice from somewhere toward the rear of the station wagon:

"How far we gotta go? How much longer this gonna take?"

"Well, the last town we were in was Healdsburg and this next one is Geyserville. After that we hit Cloverdale and from there it's about 25 miles to Ukiah. Should take an hour or so, max." I figured that settled it.

But after a pause came another question, from another kid:

"Did you say *Cloverdale?* Are we going through Cloverdale?"

I knew the kid's voice and I found his face in the rearview mirror. "Yeah, Ricky, in a few minutes we're going through Cloverdale," I said. "That OK?"

"Whoa," said Ricky. "Cloverdale? I didn't know we went through Cloverdale."

I explained it all. I explained how maps and geography and the California highway system all conspired to make it pretty difficult to reach Ukiah on 101 from the south without running through Cloverdale.

But Ricky wasn't listening. "I used to live in Cloverdale," he finally said. "I didn't know it was around here."

I knew he had been placed in the group home out of Alameda County, so I was a bit curious. "Whaddya mean, Cloverdale? I thought you used to live in Oakland."

Ricky explained how his parents got divorced a long time ago, when he was around six or seven years old, and that mom stayed in Oakland but dad moved to someplace called Cloverdale. Ricky said that about once a month dad would pick him and his brother up to spend the weekend. He hated going to Cloverdale.

"We never got to do anything because my dad was always working," he said. "He had a job at this potato chip factory and he always had to be at work when me and my brother were with him. So he'd park at the factory and go to work. We'd wait out in the car.

"We hated it. It was always so hot. Hot and boring. Me and my brother would argue and fight and then we'd go to sleep, and then about every couple hours dad would come out and give us a bag of potato chips. Or pretzels. Or whatever it was they were making in the factory. Then he'd go back to work and we'd be out there in the car waiting until he got off."

I continued driving north. I had lived in Cloverdale for a few years and knew how fiendishly hot summers could get, especially for a couple kids sitting in a car in a parking lot. But I didn't remember a potato chip factory.

By now the four lane freeway had shrunk to two lanes and Highway 101 became Cloverdale Boulevard as it went through town. I was doing maybe 20 miles an hour. We entered the city limits. I came to a stop at the only traffic light in town there at the corner at First Street. Ricky was leaning forward and he rested his arms on the back of the front seat. He looked around and tried to figure out where the potato chip factory was.

The light changed and we pulled slowly forward.

"Hey!" Ricky shrieked, about eight inches from my right ear. "Right there! Right there! The potato chip factory!"

He was looking and gesturing to his left, and I turned my head that direction. We were driving slow. There was nothing but storefronts with green awnings. I looked at where he was pointing.

"Uhh, well, gee," I said finally with a sigh. "Hate to say this, Ricky, but I'm afraid that's not a potato chip factory.

"That's Elmer's Bar."

Life's Simple Pleasures (Cont'd)

The possibility the upcoming
NFL season will be canceled

When life's got me down, when I'm
blue and depressed, it always cheers
me up when I remember that
Michael Jackson is dead

The S.S. Ukiah is taking on water

Local officials can't come to grips with the actual problems that infest our town so they spend their time and our money addressing meaningless issues and solving non-problems.

The streets of Ukiah are overrun with hopeless derelicts and violent, drug-numbed weirdies from other planets, or at least other zip codes. Every day on page two of the Daily Journal we see the Police Notes, which suggest a small sample of the problem: a man beating on dog on East Gobbi; a woman urinating on the sidewalk in front of an elementary school, a stabbing here, an assault there, a few people screaming at traffic and throwing rocks on South State Street. There's even an occasional arrest.

City and county officials do nothing, and they do nothing for two reasons. The first is that they came of age during the 1960s when drug use was regarded as a harmless, victimless rebellion against uptight middle class values. Deviant behavior was celebrated in the '60s and craziness was simply considered *different*, as in "they aren't out of their mind, they're out of your mind."

The second reason is that those in charge of the government are closely allied, politically and philosophically, with those who operate non-profit groups and government programs. These agencies supposedly exist to help those in need, but over the decades they've evolved into mere employment programs.

The reality is that if these professional uplifters and all their programs actually helped the homeless, there'd be fewer homeless. But that's not the way it works. Instead, the number of people eligible for assistance continues to grow, which means increased funding for the programs. And thus more people get hired.

Local officials wear double sets of handcuffs. They get all squeamish cracking down on the mopes and creeps that have invaded the town, and at the same time they rake in grant money by pretending to do something. If the problem goes away, the funding goes away.

The result is that the city council has all but abandoned efforts to save Ukiah, and has instead decided to save the world. How?

- Banning plastic bags, of course. Not that you could find one Ukiahan in 10 who thinks it's a priority or even beneficial.
- Buying a fleet of Priuses.
- Buying cool electronic gadgets for themselves like iPad Tablets. These are hi tech goodies that council members don't really need and that a peasant such as yourself can't afford. But taxpayers should get ready to buy a bunch for the council and its staff and anybody else who wants one at city hall.
- Planning a bicycle-friendly "corral" outside a restaurant on North School Street
- Redoing downtown intersections in fake red cobblestone.
- Hanging stupid signs on downtown light poles telling the world about our wine and cheese and art and dance, hoping to trick a stray tourist or two into spending some time in Ukiah.
- Making sure teenage boys wear six helmets apiece when they hang around the skatepark. For a council that can't control drunks vomiting on your car at Safeway it seems odd to be so intent in cracking down on a few kids bothering no one.

But that's the point. The council believes it is powerless to improve the actual quality of life in Ukiah, so it concentrates on stuff like stringing white lights through the branches of downtown trees, or debating the wars in the Middle East. Anything to avoid having to deal with the people sprawled across the steps of the Methodist Church every morning awaiting more services, more handouts and more benefits from people paid to provide programs.

And while those in charge pretend not to notice, the crazy lazy invaders continue their open air assault on the town. Our "leaders" respond with empty gestures, as if sincere, well-meaning theatrics are a worthy substitute for action. The ship is taking on water and our officials are busy checking to make sure the water is organic, shade grown and comes from local ponds.

No one thinks the city is on the right course. No one thinks those in power have a clear understanding of what's wrong with the city, much less a plan to fix things. When we have petty tyrants on our Planning Commission insisting that only government-approved artwork shall be acceptable on the exteriors of local businesses, something is wrong.

Jobs and businesses are disappearing. North State Auto is gone and so are Diversified Lending and Ukiah Valley Lumber and Cinnabar Ceramics. Businesses are being crippled and destroyed by a weak economy and foolish leaders. The Planning Commission thinks the answer is to ban new ventures like a Peet's Coffee Shop or an In-n-Out Burger outlet. There's all the usual snorting and grumbling about big corporations and entry level wages, and the dangers they pose to our precious community values and small town charms.

Well, pick up any Daily Journal and read page two. Tell me again about those values and charms and tell me again how they fit into the quality of life here in Ukiah.

Save a tree *now* !

Much of what's screwy about the local environmental crowd is presently on display over at Grace Hudson Park.

A big old dead or dying oak tree stands in the northwest corner of the yard and has become the focus of attention for our noble defenders of Mother Nature. The city has had various arborists take the old tree's pulse and all come back with the same verdict: Tree future be bad.

To an environmentalist the loss of a tree, even one that went unnoticed until the yellow warning tape went up around it, is worse than the loss of a child or a parent or a battalion of American soldiers in Afghanistan.

Nothing brings the weeping furies out of an eco-head like the potential loss of a tree. All trees are rare and endangered. This is because every tree is sacred and spiritual and a vital link in our fragile eco-system, although if any of these people were to get in a plane and spend three minutes up in the air around here they'd realize there are about as many trees in Mendocino County as there are grains of sand along the county's coast.

No matter. The envirobots are already demanding the Grace Hudson tree be spared, and in a recent front page news story they are conjuring up the usual superstitious blather about the tree being a "grandmother" and somehow critical to the hopes and dreams of Native Americans everywhere. We've all seen this rubbish before. In the near future we can expect the following:

1. Long letters filled with the same boring clichés that we haven't paid any attention to over the past 20 years will start showing up in the Daily Journal.
2. There is already talk of protesters chaining themselves to the tree, although it is surely wrong for you to hope lightning strikes the tree when they do.
3. Elderly hippie women will seize the opportunity to go topless and sing songs about the murder of a tree. I have seen these semi-naked eco-hags sing at other demonstrations and I will drive 16 blocks out of my way to not see them again.
4. Poems will be recited and George Bush will be blamed.

When at last (after either one week or until it rains, whichever comes first) the righteous indignation finally withers and the outrage dies out, all our fist-shaking progressives will go back home and join the ranks of the other silly goofs who have demonstrated around here in recent years. Let us now pause to admire the mighty achievements accomplished in recent years by our silly goofs:

The anti-war crew which used to gather in front of the courthouse but disappeared long before the war(s) did, apparently having grown tired of its own meaningless antics.

And none of us shall ever forget the courageous band of activists that promised to halt the closing of the downtown Post Office. This was a sturdy group that A) marched, B) petitioned, and C) immediately gave up.

Then we had folks all in a sweaty uproar a few years back because the new Walgreens store was going to force the execution of half a dozen trees. Not sure how that fierce struggle ended.

Next it was our Occupy Ukiah heroes, who took it to The Man a few months ago because of credit cards or bankers making less money than Hollywood celebrities or someone not being allowed to live in a house they couldn't afford.

Now it's trees again. The tree-savers all seem to overlook one inescapable fact: Trees die. All of them. So does everything else that's alive in nature. A tree lives a long and glorious life but eventually it grows old and weak and starts to die, and the answer from an environmentalist is to put the tree on life support? Buy it a dialysis machine? Begin leaf replacement surgery?

What's next—tree funerals at Eversole Mortuary and dignified burials at Low Gap Cemetery?

We live in Ukiah, and therefore Stupid is something we understand. We have lived among the nation's stupidest people ever since they all moved here from Cleveland and started their communes and health food stores. But at some point we need to take our brain-numbed, nature loving goo-goos aside and explain the realities of the world.

We can start the conversation by pointing out that there's a reason grandma doesn't send you a Christmas card anymore, which is that she's dead. And the dog you had when you were 12 years old? Dead. Also Elvis, Princess Di and Paul McCartney.

We can then move on to showing our local stupids Page Two of the Daily Journal, where things called "obituaries" are carried. We'll explain that these obituaries are "little stories about people who are dead."

Eventually we'll get around to the tree at Grace Hudson and some other trees and the trees in the forest and all the trees in the world. "They will all die some day," we'll say sadly, and perhaps Mister Eco Warrior will cry when we say this. It will be a teachable moment.

It won't be easy because these people are stupid (only a stupid person would chain herself to a dying tree, after all) and stupid is hard to fix.

Visit Lake County, Land of Enchantment

People tend to have a low opinion of Lake County. They say it has the highest percentage of parolees in the state and that it has the lowest per capita income in all of California. Perhaps true, but it also helps explain why Lake County remains value-priced for would-be vacationers in these difficult economic times. And in Lake County, remember, the difficult economic times never go away.

And don't worry about some of those distorted images of the area promoted by the media. If you think a weekend in Lake County means you'll be surrounded by criminals and poor people think again, because you'll also get to enjoy a great big polluted lake. And with your luck the entire time you're over there the J. Geils Band will be playing at that Konocti Harbor resort.

But follow me and it won't be all bad. Here are my tips for how to maximize your enjoyment on a trip to Lake County:

BEFORE YOU GO

Visit your friend who has that broken refrigerator in his garage that he's been trying to get rid of. Take it along. Lake County folks are always happy to install new play equipment in their front yards for neighborhood children.

WHERE TO EAT IN LAKE COUNTY

My wholehearted recommendation is that you dine outdoors, because there are abundant fruit and nut orchards throughout all of Lake County. So park your car, hop a fence and enjoy all the purloined pears and walnuts you can eat. (Note to Lake County residents who may be reading: "purloined" is a word that means "stolen" and can be found in a big book called a "dictionary.")

BEST BAR IN LAKE COUNTY

No question about it, the best place to drink in Lake County is a six-pack in the front seat of your car. Remember, bars in Lake County are often filled with people who live in Lake County.

REAL ESTATE IN LAKE COUNTY

Compared with housing prices in the rest of the state Lake County's truly a bargain. This is due in part because a "lakefront property" in Lake County means your front yard is full of dead fish six months of the year and drunken boaters for three. Also, be aware that when a Lake County real estate agent begins talking to you about a "gated community" she means the county jail.

FUN THINGS TO DO IN LAKE COUNTY

Bring your crackpipe. New friends will find you.

BEST FISHING IN LAKE COUNTY

I guess Safeway in Lakeport has your best seafood selection. If you're considering baiting your hook and fishing in Clear Lake, I have a better idea: Toss some carp into your toilet and trying reeling 'em in.

BEST VIEW IN LAKE COUNTY

Leave Ukiah heading east on Highway 20, take a right on Highway 29 and go south past Lakeport. After a few miles you'll see a blue sign that reads "Vista Point." This takes you to a big parking lot. Walk to the highest point, about 30 yards away. Stand there, turn 180 degrees around so you're now facing west, and if you get up on your tiptoes you should be able to see Mendocino County way off in the distance.

BEST FAMILY FUN IN LAKE COUNTY

Leave your entire family home in Ukiah. They don't need any more entertainment, do they? I mean, didn't you just finish taking them all to Pumpkinfest? Plus, you shouldn't visit your new girlfriend at the Lucerne Royale Trailer Park while your wife and kids wait outside in the Dodge Caravan.

Life's Simple Pleasures (Cont'd)

Neither of my kids has a tattoo

Spotting your ex-girlfriend's picture in the
Wedding Announcement section
and realizing she's gained 30 lbs.

Save the County, Close the libraries

If Mendocino County is strapped for money, and I believe it is, the most logical thing it could do is close down all the libraries.

Lock the doors, shut off the lights, sell the books. Rent out the buildings to Domino Pizza outlets and Verizon franchises. Turn the bookmobile into a taco truck.

Libraries are the blacksmith shops of the 21st century, obsolete relics of another era. Their time is past, as gone as the Monroe Doctrine and the Bronze Age. Today going to the library is an exercise in nostalgia, an attempt to revisit your youth, or, more probably, the youth of your grandparents. But it's easy to go years and years without visiting a library—I haven't had a library card in a quarter century and can't recall a single time I wished I had one.

I don't go to our local library partly because it doesn't stock what I read (where is the coloring book section, anyway?) and partly because it's never open at convenient times. The library schedule is strictly for the benefit of the people who work there and those who use it as a daycare option between stops at Plowshares and Ford Street. Libraries are simply one more taxpayer-funded entity in which the people who use it don't pay for it, and the people who pay for it don't use it.

Go on down to the library at the corner of East Perkins and North

Main and see for yourself. Behold: people vigorously exercising their right to ruin yet another public facility, this one dedicated to knowledge and learning, and transform it into just another pit stop for drunks and transients and people looking to bathe in public bathrooms.

The first thing you'll notice when you visit the library is that dumpster diving must be exhausting work, given the number of people who are dead asleep with their heads on the tables. And speaking of "exhausting" this place could use a fan.

The only other folks in the building are old people and hippies. Old people go to libraries out of habit, hippies go to libraries because they're free. Hippies love a free anything. If you told a bunch of hippies there was a free funeral service tomorrow afternoon at Eversole Mortuary they'd be there. Hippies would line up in the parking lot at Pardini Appliance if they heard there was going to be free admission over the weekend. Wait'll they find out about the free popcorn at Rainbow Ag.

Some will argue that we need libraries because they are centers for research and intellectual inquiry. Historically this has certainly been the case but it's no longer true. There was a revolution about 20 years ago. It was called the internet. Today any teenager can unearth more information in a five minute Google session than you could discover in five days at the library.

And the idea that society should provide free libraries so that valuable research can be conducted by serious scholars is utterly ridiculous, at least around here. There aren't three people in all of Mendocino County doing anything involving serious research at the library. Even if they were the remedy would be simple: give them each $500 to buy a laptop computer at Radio Shack. Problem solved.

The way written information is conveyed has undergone continuous changes over thousands of years. It's gone from cave paintings and stone tablets to illuminated manuscripts and scribes to moveable type and high speed presses. Now it's cyberbooks and print-on-demand. I don't know what it'll be in 10 years but it sure won't be libraries.

Spending major money today to build, maintain, and staff book warehouses for a dying technology makes no sense. Spending public dollars to fund free book distribution centers in the early 21st century is equivalent to spending public transportation dollars to fund the construction and maintenance of horse corrals in the early 20th century.

We're also going to hear that we need to keep libraries open because they provide easy access to reading material for poor people. Not true. Libraries are difficult to get to, as they require a car or bus or taxi or else a long walk in the rain, and when you finally get there it's closed due to budget cuts. Whereas I'm willing to bet that right this minute you are within a hundred feet of a computer.

The final wobbly argument in favor of keeping the libraries running is that it would prevent lost jobs among the librarian class. True enough, but if libraries have devolved to the point where they exist simply as jobs programs, then put the unemployed librarians to work picking up trash on highways or painting over graffiti or removing the ugly murals around town.

If your only job skills are a thorough understanding of the Dewey Decimal System and the ability to alphabetize, what did you expect? Tenure?

Anyway, good luck in the employment market. Learn to make a good burrito and maybe you can run the taco truck.

Look—a perfect town I don't want to live in!

You can consult any number of sources for advice about the best cities to live in or the Top Ten Retirement spots in the nation. Magazines and websites rank places all around the country by how well they score in various categories: low crime, nice weather, access to health care, affordable housing, etc.

Yet it occurred to me last week that even if your fabulous new retirement city gets high marks in all the right categories, you might still wind up in a horrible town. I imagined myself moving to some sweet village with perfect weather, an American League baseball team 40 miles away, and housing so cheap I could buy a condo on the golf course. All is swell.

But what if, on the third day, while driving to the liquor store I see a car—a Subaru, no less!—with a bumpersticker that reads "Practice Random Acts of Kindness and Senseless Beauty" or whatever those stupid things say. And what if, at the next traffic light I look around and see an office building with a sign that says "Holistic Healing Health Center"? Horrified, I'd panic. I'd wonder if I still had the receipt for that condo I bought so I could return it.

So I put together the following list. It enables a would-be newcomer to any town anywhere to check for warning signs and potential alerts that This Ain't The Place.

Here's how it works: Every city starts with 1000 points. Cities lose points based on objectionable qualities and irritating annoyances. So the next time you visit a new town with the idea that it might be your future home, get out this checklist and score accordingly:

+ 50 points off for every yoga studio within the city limits
+ 25 points off for every dog park
+ 100 points off if annual sales of white wine exceed those of beer
+ 25 points off every time someone tries to hug you during your visit
+ 25 points off if there are more kids playing on organized soccer teams than on Little League teams
+ 10 points off for each therapist listed in the local phone book
+ 25 points off if there is a Lexus dealership in town
+ 50 points off if there is a Prius dealership
+ 5 points off for every art gallery
+ 15 points off for every real estate shop in the "cute" or "quaint" revitalized downtown neighborhood. *Deduction doubled if the real estate shop replaced a hardware store, men's furnishings store or pawn shop.*
+ 10 points off for every health food store
+ 10 points off if there has been a poetry reading at a local bookstore within the past 12 months
+ 50 points off if there has been a Performance Art production anywhere inside the city limits in the past 12 months
+ 10 points off if a Hollywood celebrity has a vacation home within 20 miles
+ 5 points off for every church with a "social justice" message on a signboard in front of the building
+ 5 points off if the local newspaper carries a daily astrology feature

+ 5 points off if the local newspaper carries "The Family Circus" on its comics page

+ 5 points off for every "Question Authority" or "Question Reality" or "Kill Your Television" bumpersticker spotted

+ 25 points off if any downtown warehouse has been converted to housing lofts for artists

+ 10 points off for every self-described "progressive" holding public office

+ 15 points off if there are more tattoo parlors than bars in town

+ 20 points off if no local radio station carries broadcasts of games played by the nearest Major League team

+ 15 points off if local liquor stores don't stock Pabst Blue Ribbon beer.

Your heavenly piece of real estate is out there, my friends, it's just that you have to know where to look—and what to look out for.

Awards of Dubious Distinction, (Cont'd)

Best-Selling magazine, Ukiah Co-op

Any prize at Pumpkinfest

Just take Easy Street To Povertyville

No matter how good so-called "poor" people in this country have it, there is always a well-oiled and highly synchronized team of government agents and media alarmists who insist poor people live in desperate and horrifying conditions. But it's not true.

Anyone willing to open their eyes—even stupid people, even social workers—can see that the people in this country that we label as "poor" are clearly not poor. And despite all the sobbing and moaning and blubbering about "the growing gap between rich and poor" there is actually nothing to fear. People aren't tumbling into poverty and starving to death on the streets of Covelo or Comptche or Calpella.

We are constantly being told by gasbag politicians on CNN or pious Washington Post columnists that our nation is a nasty, intolerant and wicked one because it neglects the poor. Utter balloonjuice.

Here are some common questions about poverty in America:

QUESTION: Are poor people magicians?

ANSWER: No, it just looks that way because despite having no money, poor people all have expensive flat-screen TVs, cell phones, PlayStations, Game Boys, iPods, Blackberries and laptop computers. Also, their children (and they have a lot of children) all wear Nike shoes that cost more than your wardrobe.

Q: If poor people are so poor, why are they so fat?

A: Because they get free food from the rest of us and they eat every bit of it. Then they lick their plates. Also, poor people eat fast food by the truckload and quarts of ice cream like you eat M&Ms.

Q: What about the Safety Net that is supposed to be unraveling? I fear this is a big problem facing our nation.

A: Don't worry. Today the "Safety Net" is actually more of a hammock. Generation after generation of "poor" people have been able to relax their lives away, and then pass these skills on to their children and grandchildren.

Q: I hear about the divide between the "Haves" and the "Have Nots." Is this a growing problem?

A: I am happy to say it is not. The problem is more accurately described as one of the "Do's" and the "Do Nots." Poverty in America is almost always the result of bad behavior and stupid choices by ignorant people. It is rarely the result of institutionalized racism or selfish fellow-citizens refusing to help those in need. If you think about it realistically, regardless of the level you are able to sink to you will always find a government program (or several) to pick up the slack for you and your family.

Remember, no matter how lazy you and your family are and no matter how little you contribute to your own well-being, you will still receive an avalanche of benefits:

Free medical care, which means anytime you feel like it you can drop by the emergency room and have that toenail looked at.

Free school for (all) your kids, and when they drop out after eighth grade they can enroll in "training centers" funded by "jobs bills" via uplifting-sounding programs like "Ladders of Opportunity" and "Let No One Fail."

Free roads and free libraries and free parks and free courthouses and free social workers and free mental health workers at free clinics.

Free food from free food stamps and food banks and Plowshares and the other agencies that collect food and money for you at churches, plus more free food when you shoplift, and a free lawyer when you get caught. Then it's free meals at the jail for the next 30 days, along with free housing and more free medical care.

Free drugs through MediCal and MediCare. Reduced prices on drugs from your crack dealin', pot growin', meth usin' friends.

Free rent through Section 8 vouchers, Ford Street Program and Social Services.

Free foster care and group homes and CYA for your kids if you remember to abuse or neglect them sufficiently.

See? No matter how much poor people don't do to not help themselves and their families, there is never a shortage of programs and people to make sure no one slips through the imaginary cracks in our cold and heartless society. And don't forget that no matter how many cubic tons of services a "poor" person can wring from society, he pays zip, zero, not a thing in return.

What do impoverished folks in the good ol' USA have to do to earn such bounty? Why, two or three times a year they are required to waddle around in front of TV cameras holding up signs that say "Don't Balance the Budget on the Backs of the Poor!" and "Why Can't My Seven or Nine Child Go Harvard? It Not Fair!"

Just Say No to Helmets

About 10 years ago I figured out what the big deal is about skateboarding and why some kids (98% of which are teenage boys) are drawn to it.

It's risky and edgy of course, and I guess girls go for skatey guys who can grind and grab air. But the real lure, I think, is that skateboarding is the only outdoor activity that doesn't have a bunch of dweeby adults standing around telling kids what to do and how to do it and how much better they used to do it when they were kids.

Every other sport has a fat guy named "Coach" with a whistle around his neck. On the sidelines is a herd of nervous mothers hoping their darling little 12-year old doesn't get grass stains on her uniform pants. Every other sport has someone keeping score and someone else enforcing the rules and a hundred people in the stands yelling.But none of this happens in skateboarding. In skateboarding no one is checking the clock or asking for a timeout. Skateboarders don't have to learn complicated plays or hear all about the glorious history of the sport.

There are no skate teams or tournaments or standings. There are no mandatory workouts, and nobody yells at a skater because he's overweight or his grades aren't good. There is no danger of having your picture appear in tomorrow's Ukiah Daily Journal sports section. Skaters don't have to wear uniforms or shin guards or knee pads.

Or helmets.

This current wave of anxiety about kids at skateparks not wearing helmets is silly. All the fretting about the horrors and perils and dangers of riding a skateboard without a helmet originates from the same crybaby wing of local hysterics who get upset anytime it appears someone out there is having fun. If it isn't a kid without a helmet it's someone smoking a cigarette or eating bacon.

Helmets are stupid and dippy. The only thing a helmet accomplishes is making a goofy doofus look like an even bigger dorkola than she already is. And really, why stop at helmets just for those tooling around the streets on wheels?

Why not make your kid wear a helmet at the dinner table in case he dives off his chair when you serve eggplant? Why not make your kids wear helmets when they brush their teeth? Why not special government-approved helmets to sleep in?

Leave the skaters alone, OK? They aren't hurting you and they won't hurt themselves. If they fall they won't crack their head open because they're young and they're quick and they'll get an elbow up and crack that instead.

Forcing kids to wear helmets at skateparks is just more granny nanny nonsense from know-nothing adults who ought to go back in the house and watch more TV. Aren't there some Seinfeld re-runs you're afraid you're going to miss?

It's a tough world out there and wrapping kids up in flannel blankies so they never get hurt is moronic. Make them wear helmets at skateparks and they'll find other, crazier, things to do.

I think kids ought to take more risks, not fewer.

Kids ought to throw firecrackers at each other and dare each other to eat weird stuff (*Yes* to Tabasco Sauce, *No* to Drano). They ought to wrestle and ride their bicycles to the Mill Creek ponds and jump in. They ought to get some friends and walk out to the coast and back on the Skunk railroad tracks.

Me? I'm going to hang out at the skatepark on weekends and give out free packs of cigarettes to kids who roll without helmets.

Let's buy some real estate that we'll never even see

When it comes to wasting money, there's no better, faster way than having the government buy up huge tracts of land under the guise of "wilderness protection." I've never see one that wasn't (A) a bad idea and (B) a bad deal.

You can look at spending at the Pentagon, or the bottomless rat hole of public schools, or even the proposed Ukiah bus station for the MTA and you won't find any bigger waste of money than the idiotic purchase of so-called public lands.

Hardly a month goes by without some politician announcing that yet another million acres of land located a thousand miles north of nowhere have been bought up and roped off and saved forever.

Bought for who? Saved from what? Why? It makes absolutely no sense to take great big parcels of land that nobody is using and then fencing them off so that nobody can use them. Take as examples the semi-local purchases of the Yolla Bolly wilderness area, something called the Lost Coast, and the Headwaters thing. All were announced as mighty triumphs over greedy developers and a huge boon to the public. Utter nonsense, of course, and to prove that these kinds of deals are always and without exception completely useless wastes of money, consider the following:

1. Have you ever visited the Lost Coast wilderness area? (Yes / No)
2. Do you know anyone—a friend, a family member, an acquaintance, or someone you read about in a travel magazine within the last 10 years—who has ever visited the Lost Coast wilderness area? (Yes / No)
3. If offered a free, all expenses paid roundtrip vacation to the Lost Coast wilderness area, would you take it? (Yes / No)
4. If someone gave you $1000 in addition to that all expenses paid vacation to the Lost Coast, would you go? (Yes / No)
5. Would anyone? (Yes / No)

We already know every answer to every question. Nobody would even consider spending seven days at the Lost Coast (which I'm guessing is some kind of remote forest-type place) because we all intuitively understand it would be a terrifying experience.

The first thing that would happen when you got to Lost Coastville is that your cell phone would say "bleeup" and then go dark. Your GPS would blink a couple times before signing off. You wouldn't be able to find a motel or a restaurant within two days driving, which of course wouldn't matter anyway because you wouldn't be in a car. The environmentalists who arrange the purchase of these zillions of acres of remote properties always demand that motor vehicles be prevented from entering forever and ever. This rule helps squirrels, and also keeps people from the 21st century from visiting.

I'd run the other way if someone suggested I go the ol' Lost Coast. I'd rather spend 24 hours at Walmart than 24 minutes at the Lost Coast or at Yolla Bolly. Or the Headwaters. Or any of these other national forest lands, most of which probably haven't had a dozen visitors in 40 years.

The newest one that I know of was announced a year or so ago by Senator Dianne Feinstein, (D-Wealth) who boldly bought up (with your money) vast swaths of the Mojave Desert, thus saving those fragile lands from development by big corporations wanting to put in lakes and rivers and resorts for rich people.

Whenever these announcements are made about more acres of remote, unwanted acreage being bought up, they always come with the same underlying message: It's being done for the future. And for the planet. And for your children. And your children's children.

Right. Of course. Because if the government doesn't buy Montana, who will? And if South Dakota isn't made into a national park, we all realize it will dry up and blow away.

And as for the theory that the Lost Coast must be preserved or else my grandchildren won't get to experience the awesome majesty, well, maybe they're talking about someone else's grandchildren.

Are you planning to send your grandkids into some wilderness that's not even on a map yet? I guess they'll get parachuted in, carrying backpacks filled with trail mix and gummi bears. If you're lucky the local wolves will eat the trail mix first, which means the kids will have a head start running back home.

My plan is to give my grandchildren video games that allow them to explore all the nation's parks and wilderness areas, including the Lost Coast They'll be able to munch trail mix and shoot wolves and squirrels from the warmth and safety of grandpa's living room.

Life's Simple Pleasures, (Cont'd)

Nothing beats a heavy rainstorm the day after one
of those "Pastels in the Park" events where school kids are
forced to do huge colorful chalk drawings all over sidewalks.

Off in the distance, the long, mournful
sound of a train whistle at midnight.

Bacon.

Teach Your Dog to Shoplift

You're only as old as you think you are if you aren't thinking

Getting old used to mean you wore baggy old trousers, a polyester shirt and puttered around the yard and garden a lot. Your diet changed a little mostly because of the dentures thing.

Sometimes friends came over to play gin rummy or canasta or bridge with you and the wife. You went in for more checkups when you got old.

You sold one of the cars and kept the other because, really now, why do we need two cars if neither of us is working? You kept the remaining car in perfect condition, getting the oil changed every few months (about every 200 miles) and you bought new tires whenever the guy at the tire shop suggested it.

You took naps. You puttered in the garden some more. You watched Johnny Carson and went to bed fairly late but still got up in time to spend most of tomorrow in the garden.

Not anymore.

Today when you get old you're supposed to embrace a healthy, vibrant lifestyle. You're supposed to stay fit and eat right and run marathons. You're supposed to learn conversational Italian, go on long cruises and rekindle your love for chess and astronomy. You should learn to mix drinks with smutty names like "Stiffy on the Rocks" and "Big Oh! Gasm" and "Viagra Falls with a Twist."

Haven't read Proust? Never a better time! Don't know how to dance the tango? There are classes at the college four nights a week for active go-getters like you!

After all, 65 is the new 30 and so when you get enough birthdays under your belt you should go live in a gated somewhere with six golf courses, bike paths everywhere and a clubhouse that has 20 TVs, shuffle-board and a schedule of daily activities led by an exuberant 20-year old fitness instructor. Calisthenics can be fun and challenging, after all. It's all part of an active lifestyle.

Well, no thanks. Where's the hammock? Mow my lawn for me. I don't know how many cars I've got and I don't care because I lost my keys last week.

I don't want to go on a cruise anywhere except maybe the liquor store. I don't want my 65 to be 30 and I don't even want it to be 64. I got where I am the old-fashioned way and that's the direction I plan on going.

You can go to an amusement park and ride the Screaming Death Drop of Doom and then play miniature golf and drink a Tequila Hottie. Next, drive home in your Porsche Excita. Won't matter to me. I'll be asleep when you get here anyway.

When did all this idiocy start, anyway? When were we supposed to not act our age and instead pretend we're younger than our children? Do you honestly think I'm going to put on a disco costume and a wig and tell people I roll wi' da hip hop?

The line is being drawn and I'm sure you know which side of it I'm on.

It's all more baby boomer baloney. My generation has all the stupidest ideas in history and this is just the latest. And maybe the worst.

No, wait. This isn't the worst. The worst one was probably the puka shell necklace thing. Or maybe it was James Taylor. Or "Tune In, Turn Over, Drop Dead" slogans. Or pet rocks or heavy metal. Or maybe it was Jonathan Livingston Seagull or macramé, or drumming circles or astrology or sand candles or the Plastic Ono Band.

Maybe it was McGovern for President or smiley face buttons or Gloria Steinem or Froot Loops or ergonomic chairs. Might have been the Back to the Land movement or self-esteem or the i-ching, or else it was Che Guevara or Richard Simmons or tie-dye t-shirts or alternative anything.

Shut up—I'm not done. Maybe the worst idea of my generation was "underground" newspapers or maybe it was Woodstock or else compost toilets or Kumbaya or free love or tattoos on the neck or going to events dressed in your underwear or therapy. Yeah, it probably was therapy.

And now they want us to embrace the healthy new world of geezerhood by pretending we're all oblivious? You go ahead and join an Active Senior Club. Get some botox while you're up, and a facelift and some hair transplants and don't forget to cap your teeth. You'll look so young and so great. Everyone will think you were born yesterday. Or maybe they'll think you fell off a nearby turnip truck.

Go on a cruise and then come home and put pushpins in a map to show people all the places you've been that you can't pronounce or remember? For what? Climb rocks? Why? If I thought I had to strap on a helmet and ride a bicycle to the yogurt shop I'd go to a nursing home instead.

Thinking you'll stay juicy and youthy with yoga and pilates is a sure sign of feeblemindedness and dementia.

Stick with the crossword puzzles is my advice, and if those are too difficult try a coloring book. Get your niece to help you pick out the crayons. Making a big ball out of rubber bands is hobby enough for me.

Now is the time to relax and get out of the way. Don't go taking up part-time work in order to "stay involved" because all you're really doing is keeping a teenager from having her first job. Besides, teenagers working are what pay your Social Security.

Go out on the porch and check the temperature a few times a day. Keep a small binder where you can record daily rainfall amounts. It might come in handy for someone's research in a couple decades. Have your oil changed again.

Avoid people who look fabulous, dress to kill and do tai chi. Write letters to your kids. Don't forget to feed the cat.

Treat your kid just like a dog

About ten years ago we (wife Teri, son Lucas and I) were sitting around the living room reading. The dog sauntered in.

"Oh is that my little puppykins?" asked Teri in a cheerful tone. "Is that my little Snuppy? Good Snuppy, good Snuppy!"

The dog jumped up on the sofa and I scratched her belly and growled happily at her. "Dassa good dog! Good dog! You want a treat?" And I dug into a pocket and pulled out a crunchy the size of a dime. She wolfed it down and drooled a load of dogspit onto my pant leg.

And watching from across the room was Lucas, arms folded and silent. He saw the entire pathetic scene play out.

"So," he said evenly, "How come no one cares when I walk through the door? Why doesn't anybody get all excited and tell me what a good boy I am and scratch me behind the ears and give me a cookie every time I come into the room?

"All the stupid dog did was walk in the door. You two act like she's made it back from a journey over frozen tundra to bring serum to dying children. Why not throw a party for me every day when I get home from Pomolita?"

Lucas was 11 and he had a point. He always does.

We've pretty much lost our way when it comes to our relationships with dogs. We treat our dogs like celebrities or minor deities. We treat our kids like furniture.

These days people celebrate their dogs' birthdays. Dogs are fashion accessories and people imagine that they have meaningful relationships with them. We arrange play dates for dogs and take them to special recreation areas to frolic and jump and learn bad behavior and leave steaming piles on the ground which we hurry over to clean up with our special little plastic baggies.

We pick up their poo for them. Is it any wonder your dog thinks she's special when she has a personal assistant to clean up after her? It's more than Donald Trump's valet does.

Why don't we start wiping their south end with specially moistened doggie towelettes infused with the fresh aroma of veal stew? Of course now that I've mentioned it some batty old (well, middle-aged) lady living on Ukiah's west side will start providing that very service for her dog Clooney.

Are we sick? Are we crazy?

Isn't allowing a dog inside the house and feeding it twice a day enough? Do we really have to invite him up on the sofa or onto the bed? Do we really have to give them 'people' names like Max and Rosie so that everyone knows we think our stupid mutt is part of the family?

Do we really have to hire consultants to whisper to our dogs?

I hear there are spas for our dogs now, and I really don't want to know the details, but I wouldn't be surprised if they included massages and teeth whitening and pedicures and cosmetic surgery. Those dogs probably keep journals. Their meals are prepared by a guy named Wolfgang Pup.

Dogs go to these spas when their owners (oops, sorry: "Guardians") are out of town. It's no longer enough to have a neighborhood kid drop by to feed Paris the Poodle and take her for a walk; only licensed, certified dog spa counselors and canine therapists are sufficient here in the 21st century.

Ukiah has built more dog parks in the past two years than skateparks in 25 years. Thankfully dogs don't live to be 25 or we'd have people wanting them to be eligible for Social Security.

I see dogs in commercials on TV and in magazine ads, promoting everything from breakfast cereal and headache remedies to bathroom cleansers and laptop computers. People now base their decisions on what brand of lawn mower or breath freshener to buy based on the breed of dog shown in commercials.

Are we crazy? Are we sick?

I think the trend is irreversible. That doesn't mean individuals can't rebel and start having their dogs stay outside except at night when they can sleep in the laundry room. Purina chow is fine. Dogs don't need rhinestone collars or special $100 toys or their picture taken with Santa.

And next time your kid comes into the room scratch him behind the ears and say "Ooh, dassa big boy! Dassa good boy!" to him

Tell him his shoes look nice. Take him for a walk.

Give him a biscuit.

Awards of Dubious Distinction, (Cont'd)

First place, annual Willits Meth Cook-off

Headline act, Ukiah Sundays
in the Park concert series

Thinning the Herd

This is what I dream of when I dream of a better world. This is how I want the future to be.

Let's do the following:

- People with severe health problems should be encouraged to seek out therapists, New Age healers and self-help gurus for treatment.
- Repeal motorcycle helmet laws.
- Give parents the option of not having their children vaccinated.
- Provide state and federal grants to establish massive sweat lodge construction programs all across the nation.
- Gangsta violence between Nortenos, Mafia members, Bloods, Surenos and Crips should be encouraged. (Law enforcement officials shall be required to provide free supplies of ammunition, along with maps to the homes of gang rivals.)
- Families with children facing terminal illnesses should be advised to rely on prayers and religious faith to heal them.
- Urge citizens to vigorously exercise their First Amendment right to express their thoughts and beliefs by wearing Confederate flag regalia to rap concerts, staging pro-Castro demonstrations in Miami, and anti-Obama ones in Chicago.
- Force major health care providers to expand reimbursement coverage for any treatment involving healing circles, positive thinking classes

or crystal therapies.

- Remove all barriers to suicide (start with the Golden Gate Bridge).
- In cases of life-threatening diseases, the U.S. Surgeon General should recommend hot yoga, chakra therapy and visualization techniques.

See the beauty? Do you appreciate the pure, naked genius? Understand the immense public benefit that would result if all of them—or even a sizeable number of them—were to be implemented?

It's so obvious it almost knocks you down. If people are stupid enough to go along with the above suggestions they will die sooner. Since only stupid people join gangs, leap off bridges or consult with dog whisperers, they should be encouraged, not educated.

It's Advanced Darwinism: You can either go to some phony-granola moron who promises to fix you via the healing power of laughter, or you can go to the emergency room and get some antibiotics. One choice you die, the other you live. I think we owe it to ourselves and to society to encourage stupid people who believe in auras and holistic massage to follow their dreams. Let them exercise their free spirited wisdom, and then let them die.

This is the point, of course. These are the people I want dead.

These are the people I am no longer willing to share the planet with.

Just imagine a universe—a sweet, sweet, functional and happy universe without therapists, bikers or New Age nitwits! No children of parents so stupid they don't inoculate their kids against polio and tuberculosis! I say we get rid of them by giving them choices that, since they're stupid, they will gladly embrace.

CHORUS
It's a happy healthy healing world
It's a life-affirming place
We all have Guardian Angels
To help us run our race

Let's join hands—make a circle!
In the lodge we will freely sweat
And later all drink organic green tea
And then play Russian Roulette!

Won't you join me? Can't we set aside our differences and work together toward a world with a brighter future, a world where children will grow up happy, free, and vaccinated, and the rest grow up dead?

Call Congressman Mike Thompson in his Napa office (707-226-9898) and tell him you want a federally funded sweat lodge in Ukiah. And how about another in Talmage? And Holistic Healing Centers in Willits, Boonville, Philo, and Legget, along with the repeal of motorcycle helmet laws, and ... well, you get the idea.

I'm young and dumb
and I want a tattoo

I hate to be the one to spoil all the fun these kids are having by decorating themselves, but some adult has to tell them this tattoo thing will come to no good.

The trend has just gone on too long. What started out as a minor and semi-harmless fad in the 1990s was supposed to fade out. This has not happened. Time to step up and tell the kids (and a whole lot of adults who ought to know better) that the entire sorry business is a mistake.

Tattoos ought to be just another inconsequential social trend, like shag carpet or shag haircuts or asking people "What's your sign?" at parties. This has not been the case, and the problem is that tattoos having staying power.

That hodgepodge of Japanese hieroglyphics you had stenciled (forever!) on your shoulder, and which you think means "Love Is The Peace Of Wide River Peace" but which actually says "Frtz Trpa Gaoprx-mti" will still be on your shoulder when you're my age. Except your flabby old skin will have sagged and the tatt will be down around your elbow.

Tattoos once meant things to people and society. Long ago, a tattoo might mean you are pledging everlasting love and loyalty to your mother or to your girlfriend or to the US Navy. Or a tattoo might simply mean you work at the carnival running the Tilt-o-Puke ride. But today a tattoo means you have a tattoo.

A tattoo makes you just like everybody else including your mother, your girlfriend, the carnie worker and the entire U.S. Navy. Thinking you're special because you have a tattoo is like thinking you're special because you have a Toyota.

The thrill is gone, kids. The hip, rebellious image is no more. Nobody thinks you look dangerous because you got "Out of Control" inked across your chest. Nobody thinks you suddenly got sexy because you had a crooked tattoo of a butterfly installed just north of your butt.

And no one except cops, DAs and parole officers think you're making a good career move when you get "Mexican Mafia" tattooed across your forehead.

Tattoos are for loser trash morons who haven't figured out yet that they aren't going to be 23 years old forever, or even for another six months. Tattoos are for people who are so stupid they don't realize that even their own children will eventually size mom and dad up as idiots for getting all those tattoos before they had kids, except for the new Raiders tattoos they both got last week.

You say you're 19 years old and you want a tattoo? I know the perfect one to get: a lick-n-stick tattoo from a gumball machine in the Walmart lobby. A Smurfs tattoo would be ideal. Your friends will get the joke, and your parents will thank you.

So will your children.

Gimme that old-time global warming religion

Any time the topic of religion is raised around Mendocino County you know you're not more than six seconds away from one of your neighbors or colleagues uttering the following sentence:

"Oh, I don't mind religion or whatever it is that those morons seem to think, it's just that I don't want them telling me what I should believe. I don't want anyone cramming that stuff down my throat."

This establishes the speaker as a deeply intellectual, free-thinking sort, tolerant of others while maintaining his or her own rigorous independence. The words are always said with a sort of grim conviction, perhaps to indicate the level of suffering the person has endured at the hands of religious zealots relentlessly indoctrinating others with their crazy religious beliefs.

But I don't think I've heard any serious religious talk around Ukiah within the last 25 or 30 years. I mean, who has? When did someone on a bus or a street corner or cocktail party or Little League game last try to engage you in a Bible-related conversation of any sort?

Has anyone quoted the Great Sky Father or John the Baptist or Leviticus? Has anyone suggested you might check out some chapter of the Bible as a source of information? And if they have, is this what we mean by "cramming that stuff down my throat"?

If there are people who come up and harangue folks about the miracle of Deuteronomy or the keen insights of one gospel passage or another, they sure don't live around here. I know, because I do live around here and people like that do not live around here. You'd be more likely to encounter someone trying to convince you that the earth is flat than that the words of St. Christopher have relevance to your life. For every person who talks passionately about Jesus, I'll bet there are 10,000 who talk passionately about the Giants.

However, if you want to hear pushy people scolding you you've come to the right county. Just talk to an environmentalist for three minutes. A modern day eco-nut is passionate and convinced of his beliefs and his mission, and won't mind at all cramming these righteous beliefs right down your throat.

Because if you think some guy in a tie and a short sleeve white shirt who shows up on your porch to hand you a Watchtower Magazine is "cramming that stuff down your throat," wait'll you catch the act of a global warming enthusiast.

Any environmentalist worth his carbon footprint knows how much damage we're doing to the planet and the price we're going to have to pay. The oceans will rise, the mountains will collapse and the North Pole will melt. A day of reckoning is at hand, oh ye drivers of diesel trucks, and only the righteous shall survive.

Yeah man, the end is near. Must it rain for 40 nights and 40 days to convince you that global warming is real and the end is nigh? Hurricanes and lightning and tomorrow's weather forecast are all signs that we have failed to keep our promises to our fragile planet. We're all doomed.

The mighty and the powerful, living in their fancy homes with heat and electricity and running water and air conditioning, will one day be brought low. They shall suffer. Their day of judgment is near, and the fact they once jetted to Europe for two weeks of carefree vacation will be held against them. They must repent. They must live like environmentalists in solar powered huts with woodstoves, and pedal around on bicycles while wearing beanies with pinwheels on their heads. It is the only way to salvation for us, and for Mother Earth.

When you boil it down, environmental projections and pronouncements pretty much mimic Biblical prophesy. The old-time religious whack-os have been reincarnated as environmental zealots and you get the same maniacal outlook and intolerant mindset from both. And both are absolutely convinced on the righteousness of their way.

Christian kooks used to warn of fire and brimstone. Enviro kooks warn of future droughts across fertile farmland, and Malibu flooded under 60 feet of water. Pretty apocalyptic, huh?

Christians say only those who walk in Jesus' footsteps will be saved, and only they shall inherit the earth. Environmentalists say only those who walk lightly on the earth and who recycle religiously will be able to save the earth.

I mean, I'm okay with all this. I just wonder why the Christers get the old "don't try cramming any of your nonsense down my throat" and the eco-warriors get a free pass, an invitation to speak at the high school and yet another feature story celebrating their heroics in tomorrow's newspaper.

Awards of Dubious Distinction (Cont'd)

Lifetime Achievement Award, Ukiah Architect Association

Walmart Employee Spirit Award

Opening night in Willits (!?!)

A number of years ago my life was in its usual shambles and my nonexistent job wasn't so hot either. By coincidence my unemployed brother, Petey Wayne, and an old pal, Dick Shoemaker, who taught college English (but had the summer off) were visiting.

I was living on North Oak Street at the time and the three of us began hatching a little scheme to have some fun and perhaps make some money. Keep in mind that we were drinking a lot back in those days, though Dick was older and should have known better.

We got rolling on how we could put together this little skit, like something that would maybe get us on MTV or else David Letterman, or at least be a way to meet some babes.

Theoretically. In reality we wound up being chased out of a bar in Willits and flinging our clothes onto the roof so the angry crowd in hot pursuit wouldn't recognize us.

But to get to that point in the story we have to go to the beginning. Back then, best buddy Kip was clocking a lot of stool time at John's Place up in Willits. He talked to a bartender about his friends doing a show some night; the guy shrugged and agreed. We rehearsed a little in the basement of Dick's house in Berkeley.

A week or two later we were at John's Place around 9 o'clock on a

Thursday night to see if we had a future in show biz. Kip stood on a chair, and bellowed "Ladies and Gentlemen! Please welcome . . . The Aristocrats!" and swept his arm in a wide arc toward the corner.

The stage at John's Place was a small raised platform a few inches higher than the linoleum dance floor. I think there was some kind of sheet or curtain, and when it was pulled aside, this is what the 20 or so bar patrons saw:

Dick Shoemaker—a college professor in real life, remember—is sitting on a standard wooden kitchen-type chair. He's got a rumpled corduroy sport coat on, the kind with patches on the elbows. He's whitened his beard and presents the cheerful demeanor of a doddering old coot.

Perched on each knee is a ventriloquist dummy, one dressed in short pants with suspenders and wearing a beanie with a propeller on top. On Dick's other knee is a dummy who looks pretty much like Huck Finn, complete with bare feet and straw hat.

Except they weren't dummies. They were us. Me and my brother. We were wearing costumes that might look OK on kids 40 years younger than us, and a hundred pounds lighter. We had drawn big freckles on our face with eyebrow pencil, and then added thick vertical lines down from the corners of our mouths to our chins.

Get it? A couple middle-aged guys dressed up like puppets sitting on the knees of an elderly gent who's pretending to manipulate our gestures and utter our words.

Now that you get it, do you think it's funny? Well, that's what we're in Willits to find out.

He had his hands up the backs of our shirts, or at least that's how it looked to the bar patrons. He grinned and bobbed his head and said "Mighty good to be here!" and bobbed his head some more. Petey Wayne then dropped his jaw straight down and shouted "Howdy folks!" while Dick twitched his own lips a bit. I did something pretty much the same, with Dick nodding and smiling and pretending to say my words.

We did about 10 or 15 minutes of stuff borrowed from Abbott and Costello, Sophie Tucker, Amos 'n' Andy and then we tried a Frank Sinatra medley. Midway through a mangled version of "Stairway to Heaven" Petey and I started arguing.

A ventriloquist can't handle two voices at once, of course, but the dodgy ol' perfesser wasn't thrown a bit. In fact, that's when he reached down and pulled a bottle of beer out of the ice chest on the floor and drained it. His dummies squabbled on. Next he took a sandwich from a jacket pocket and began to eat it, still pretending to lip synch along with his semi-berserk dummies.

Which is around the time it went off the rails. Petey Wayne left the script behind; he called attention to a woman sitting at the corner of the bar, suggesting her jeans were a bit tight, and that he had some ideas on fixing how ugly she was. Her boyfriend appeared to be a biker and he also appeared to be standing up.

The bartender glared at us.

Dick flipped him off.

Commotion.

I heard something break. Kip was out the front door first and I was about six feet behind him. Dick and Petey Wayne made a feint toward the bathroom, then zipped out the back door. We started pulling our clothes off and flinging them skyward as we ran for the parking lot. Angry Wilipinos were rumbling behind us. Semi-naked, we sprinted to the van, smoked the rear tires, and headed back to Ukiah.

We left behind some broken chairs, an unpaid bar tab and Dick's ice chest with a few beers still in it.

But if you find yourself in Willits someday and feel like climbing up on the roof at John's Place, I'd be willing to bet you'd find an old beanie, a straw hat and a corduroy sport coat up there.

Complaint Generation

Citizens from my generation complain about everything. Everything. Here are some favorite subjects they have wet themselves over since around 1965:

1. The Establishment. This means their parents and government, which haven't done enough for them and never will.

2. White sugar, white rice and white flour. Seriously. Something about vitamins, I guess.

3. White people (See "Establishment," above). This is because white people enslave the rest of the world, steal all the resources, and make everyone watch Gilligan's Island re-runs.

4. Police officers, or "Pigs" as they were commonly known when I was younger. My generation hated all cops, and to prove it they marched around cities and burned them down (Detroit, Newark, Cleveland and parts of LA have never recovered). Completely understandable because they were angry about violence in Amerikkka.

5. Medicine. I've been hearing the bitter complaints for 40 years about how doctors only treat symptoms. "But our bodies are organisms," they say, "and everything is interrelated and must be viewed holistically." This means if I have a heart attack I want

the attending physician to also check my toenail fungus and that itchy spot on my elbow.

6. The war in Vietnam.
7. Suburbs. (See "White people," above.) Suburbs are full of dull conformists and symbolic of all that's wrong in the world.
8. Corporations. This is the big one. Corporations are the malignant evil force lurking behind unhappiness in the universe. Every single thing the average citizen eats, wears, drives, lives in, reads and experiences is somehow linked to a corporation. Corporations obviously benefit each and every one of us. "But corporations make money!" they explain. Oh.

Reviewing the list I'll give the angry complainers Number 6. They were right about Vietnam. This means they're barely batting .100, which is proof they are stupid.

Bear in mind all this fierce anger comes during an era of unrivaled wealth and well-being. No one you know has ever missed a meal. Anyone can book a flight to Paris on less money than they earn in a paycheck. Heated homes with solid roofs, air conditioning, microwaves and TV are the norm, even at the economic bottom. The poorest, most poverty-soaked guy in 21st century America lives better than any king from pre-1900. But the sniveling never stops. Catastrophe looms. Corporate rule is coming!

It never stops and it never will. The goal is always the same: more meddlesome nonsense from people with nothing else to do, which is an excellent definition of the average modern American liberal.

Now they have a new target: GMOs. The crybabies want pure, simple, natural food just like it was grown in 1850. They want us to rally behind Prop 37, yet another food labeling requirement and probably the first step in banning GMOs altogether.

But given the track record that the people angry about genetically modified food have compiled over the years, do you think it likely their views are correct? Would you trust that the next big thing these people decide to complain about is something you should fear?

It is simply beyond dispute, and even beyond rational argument to think the agriculture industry is destroying the planet or harming the people. Food is more plentiful today than it has even been in the history of mankind. Starvation is very nearly a thing of the past and has been eradicated in almost every corner of the globe. Poor people now suffer from obesity. *Please read that last sentence again.*

We feed more people using fewer farmers than ever. And what does Complaint Generation have to say? "No! Stop! It's made from plutonium and it's radiated and your kids will be born with six toes and we need more laws and more regulations. Stop!"

Attentive readers may recall we've done all this before. Remember Prop 65 back in the 1990s? It notified you that chemicals exist at gas stations and inside boxes of fertilizer. Feel safer now? Have the number of deaths in your family gone down as a result?

Next was new and improved warning labels on cigarettes. Before that, I guess everyone thought cigs were a healthy alternative to carrot sticks.

Maybe you remember the Bad Old Days when everybody in this country was fat. Then our progressive do-gooders forced fast food joints to print calorie totals on menus. Now we all look like Paris Hilton.

The proggies say labeling GMOs will make those dangerous foods safer. People will be alerted to the radiation levels and aware of their horrors. But folks may want to remember that more people died from toxins in one (1) organic garden than have ever died from all the genetically modified foods produced in history. Let's review.

Total GMO-related deaths since the beginnings of time: Zero.

Deaths from one organic garden: Thirty.

Doesn't matter. Liberals will continue to shriek and moan and accuse GMOs of being "frankenfoods." It's always the same: lies, hysterical exaggerations and accusing opponents of being rich, sneaky and underhanded.

They cheat and distort and call their opponents nasty names. But at least their cause is righteous and their goal is noble.

The Iron Man of Redwood Valley

QUESTION: What would you get if you spent 54 years in a small grocery store stocking shelves, stacking boxes, pumping gas and sweeping floors?

ANSWER: If you were lucky you might get a day honoring you like Ralph McDill had last week out at the Redwood Valley Community Church, where hundreds gathered to pay tribute to him. It was truly an honor, and Ralph earned it the old fashioned way.

I suppose it's the 54 years working at the store that people have trouble understanding. To spend six decades in a small store in a nowhere town seems only theoretically possible, an implausible scenario in an improbable existence.

The Redwood Valley Store can't be any bigger than 2000 square feet, and almost every square inch of it is taken up by racks and shelves and products and display cases. Then there are the aisles, of course, and that's where Ralph McDill spent most of his life.

Think of all those early mornings opening up the store, and all those late nights closing it back down. Think of all the loaves of bread that needed stacking on wire racks and all the cases of Cokes and Camels and cans of tuna on all those shelves. Jars of pickles and bags of chips, cold cases filled with lunchmeat and milk.

But the day didn't end when the last customer left and the lights went out and Ralph hung up his green apron. Ralph wasn't just the guy from the Redwood Valley grocery store, since he was just about as well known around town for his volunteer work at the Community Church and at the fire department. Ralph McDill was The Mayor, after all. His impact was felt all around the valley, and in some cases well beyond it.

One fellow who'd known him since the 1960s said Ralph "wore out at least one truck" making his annual treks (two weeks at a time) to Mexico rebuilding and bringing water to some little town I'd never even heard of.

Ralph kept up lawns and tended roses for others. He visited folks in nursing homes and convalescent hospitals, and he prayed for those overwhelmed by the cards life had dealt them. A woman at the Sunday tribute told me "Ralph is amazing—sometimes I think that helping people is what the Good Lord put him on Earth to do."

Helping people? A man stood at the microphone and told the crowd about the time he mentioned to Ralph that he needed a trench dug at his home. The next day he woke up to the sound of digging, and when he looked out his side window he saw Ralph McDill busy with a shovel.

But those good deeds and selfless acts have a way of winding back to the Redwood Valley Store. Ralph told me he started work there in 1954, a time when a teenager didn't need a government permit to do a day's work.

His first task, recalled Leo Bleier Jr., son of store proprietor Leo Bleier who hired Ralph, was the job of rinsing out bottles in the back room. It generally took nearly an hour but Ralph finished in half that time, with the added bonus of having sorted and stacked the bottles according to their manufacturer. Leo the Elder knew he had a keeper in young Ralph McDill.

He didn't just give Ralph a paycheck, though. The boss taught his new stockboy to drive a car by putting him at the wheel of the family's yellow Chrysler. He taught him the value of hard work, the importance of giving to others, and helped him open his own savings account. One thing he couldn't give him was an education; Ralph never obtained his high school diploma.

So when Ralph approached the microphone in his natty blue suit last Sunday no one was expecting him to recite Shakespeare. And he didn't. Ralph spoke to the crowd the only way he knew how: from the heart and to the point.

He remembered when Mister Bleier had offered him his first job all those decades ago, and he remembered telling him "I have to ask my step-mom first." And Ralph talked about how proud he was to help raise money for the cancer society, and how much it meant to him when he was appointed Grand Marshall of the Black Bart parade.

At the end he paused and he took a deep breath. "You know," he said, "I never dreamed of this day happening. And here it is."

I suppose that not everyone in the crowd had a tear in their eyes, but I do know that everyone stood up and applauded for a long, long time. They were saying thank you to Ralph McDill. They were saying *thank you* to a man well loved, and a life well lived.

Awards of Dubious Distinction (Cont'd)

Real Estate Agent of the Year, Laytonville, CA

Top vote-getter,
Willow Waster District election

A whiter shade of pale, whitish white

I bought an old beater of a house on North Oak Street back in the '80s, fixed it up to my exacting standards and lived there happily enough, given that it was Ukiah, for more than a decade.

Then the new wife moved in, had a quick look around and called a real estate agent. It took a while but she found her dream house which, as they say, needed work. Or perhaps a bulldozer. The house was a collapsing pile of shingles and boards with a leaky roof, smelly carpets, an ugly kitchen with hilarious linoleum, and two horrid bathrooms, one of which made her cry.

So of course we bought it. The first time we walked through we realized it was a long-term project and agreed that painting it would be our first priority. "Gotta paint this," we'd murmur in unison as we stood side-by-side marveling at the old dull, dim walls.

Interior paint appeared to have last been applied sometime in the 1960's, and in a color that was probably discontinued shortly thereafter. It was a monstrous shade of curdled, earth-tone bile with a rich bouquet of must and dust. Maybe it was simply filth, which the house had plenty of; ask me sometime about the upstairs carpets soaked in cat urine, which is another story about our new house but not a very funny (ha ha) one.

There were a few other things that weren't funny, like the diseased hot tub we threw out along with the broken dishwasher, broken refrigerator and the broken water heater. Everything else was merely ugly and weird.

But this column isn't really about household projects and how long we took to complete them. It's about paint. After five years of refinishing floors and repairing decks, the living room and dining room walls remained that same mutant shade of yellowed tubercular phlegm. We could hardly stand to look at them, which meant we had to do something.

So we went to the paint store. Actually we went to maybe half a dozen paint stores. Eventually I dropped out of the paint-store-rounds and merely inspected the color chips Teri would bring home. "These all look fine," I'd say as she spread sheet after sheet of color choices in front of me. "Far as I'm concerned the walls can be polka dot."

"Oh no," said Teri. "They have to be white. A nice off-white"

Off-white is a range of color I'm OK with. I pointed to an entire page of whitish paint chips in her Sherwin-Williams booklet. "Hmmmm," she said.

Weeks went by, then months, and pretty soon it was a year. And another. I cleared my throat and suggested that perhaps 2006 might be a most opportune time to apply fresh paint. She asked what color; I again agreed to anything on the color wheel, including oranges and purples.

"I don't think so," said Teri. "I'm thinking white."

Then she called in a design consultant, Dame Judith. After a week or so walking back and forth through the living room and dining room (a roundtrip distance of about 12 feet) Dame Judith announced that she, too, favored a creamy style of white.

Gee. Wow. White? Ya think?

(*Note: Why doesn't the government require a background check and a three-day waiting period before allowing interior designers to be hired?*)

So Teri and Dame Judith huddled and murmured and pored over hundreds—nay, thousands—of white color chips, except in reality not a single one of them was white. They were all Polar Fizz and Peruvian Flake and Crème le Champagne, never just plain old white. Some stores had paints available in tiny little cans so the color could be applied directly to the walls, which Teri did.

This allowed the two designing women to ponder just how Moonbeam Cloud looked at 7 a.m. with the morning sun slanting in, versus how it looked at 4 p.m. And by "how it looked" I mean hue and tint and value and shade and tone in the vast spectrum of the color of white. So evaluate away! Then they analyzed everything all over again at 8:15 p.m. in order to determine how Moonbeam Cloud looked when viewed in the reflected glow of a 60-watt incandescent bulb.

I wish I was making this stuff up.

Tomorrow new paints (Shalimar Breeze and Fainting Spell Mist) will be applied to the walls, checked in various lights, and then re-examined. Teri and Dame Judith will cluck and mutter, they'll furrow their brows and purse their lips, and announce that all—all!—are unworthy! Next they'll wonder if the Kelly-Moore line might have something a little more ethereal than Martha Stewart's brand.

Dear readers, it's been 14 years. We've done nothing. It might be half a century since anyone laid a coat of fresh paint on these tired, filthy walls. I swear that if we haven't painted them by October I'll start hanging up bed sheets.

I think my wife has a syndrome or something. Maybe she needs help. Dame Judith? Don't care. In fact I'm thinking of getting a restraining order against her.

Farewell, Daylight Savings Time, hello misery and gloom forever

Almost nothing honks me off more than Daylight Savings Time or, more to the point, the end of it. Who is behind this? Who thinks the answer to the gloom setting into our lives is an increase in *darkness?*

The sun sinks lower, the light gets dimmer, and a dank depression settles over the land. Dreary days merge into endless nights and the American spirit droops. Our misery and grief index rises. Bleak becomes the norm. Psychic despair slowly sweeps the nation. And yet some anonymous bunch of wizards out there thinks the solution is for us all to "Fall Backwards"?

So the night comes sooner day after day. We have more darkness in our lives and it comes earlier with every tick of the calendar. Heading your way, starting this morning, is a near-terminal gray fog of drab dark dullness. And some rain. Also, expect heavy clouds and thundershowers. Clearing, with some scattered sunshine, is in our forecast for maybe next June.

Get out your parka and an umbrella or two. Lose your sunglasses. Go find yourself a copy of Finnegan's Wake. Contemplate suicide.

And if you think the prospect of nonstop soggy days blending seamlessly into cold rainy night isn't quite enough misery, add the repeal of Daylight Savings Time to your list.

Losing Daylight Savings Time means the brightest portion of your day will be when you take your morning shower. It only gets worse and darker from there. By the time you dry yourself off, make some coffee and feed the cat, the sun is already sinking off behind the trees to the west. Go back to bed. Call in depressed.

For whom does this make sense, anyway? We've been told since we were kids that Daylight Savings is farmer-friendly because it allows the yeomen of the soil to experience the warm glow of sunshine as he begins his toils each morning. Which is a grand theory. Except it's baloney.

There aren't any farmers anymore. Go look for yourself. Leave tomorrow morning (watch out for that blinding sun screaming up over the hills to the east) and drive anywhere you want. Look for farmers cheerfully pitching hay and milking cows and waving at you from behind the wheel of their John Deere tractors as they plow their jolly furrows.

But they don't because they're gone. Farmers, I mean. The reality is that no one has milked a cow by sitting on a three-legged stool at 5 in the morning and yanking on an udder since about 1950. Cows get milked by machines. The machines are made in factories. In the dark, probably.

Hay? I think all the hay and straw and stuff gets processed into brick bundles by modern equipment out in the field. And I don't think I've seen someone driving an actual John Deere tractor in so long that I'm not sure they make 'em anymore. If they do, I'll bet ol' Mister Deere sells 5000 lawnmowers for every tractor.

The short of it is that there aren't any farms or farmers left. In Mendocino County small farms have gone the way of Wildberger's Market and Lee's Fast Food. Farms are all agribusiness these days, so tell me again: Without farms or farmers what is the point of this Daylight Savings Time?

If present day crops are planted by plow / furrow / seed machine and then six months later harvested by some contraption the size of the JC Penney building, who cares if the work is done in pitch dark or with the rosy fingers of dawn slipping over the machine's hulk? And if there are no remaining farmers that we have to appease or coddle, why are we inflicting enormous black clouds of despair on the rest of us?

I say we repeal Daylight Savings Time. Better yet, let's reverse it. Every year around this time why don't we Spring Forward with our collective

Teach Your Dog to Shoplift

clock? Why don't we extend the bright cheery joys of daylight further into our bleak lives? Why don't we add an hour of sunshine to our existence once every year?

Consider the annual benefits. Adding an hour of sunlight might not sound like much right now, but imagine how much better and brighter the world (or at least Ukiah) will be by 2020. The sun will be popping over the eastern hills around midnight.

Think of the boon to downtown merchants and the increase in bonus shopping hours. Kids can play sports all night long thanks to this revolutionary legislation. And according to my calculations, if we keep adding more hours of sunshine every year pretty soon we'll be able to harvest our crops before we plant them.

Am I looking at the right calendar? Is this clock accurate?

Awards of Dubious Distinction (Cont'd)

All-time best Spencer Brewer CD

Best Local Jobs Creation Plan

MVP, Ukiah Men's B-5 Slow-Pitch League

Our new puppy: Bite! Bark! Run!

Went out and got us a new puppy a while back but at this point we can't quite remember why we did. Why would anyone bring a berserk little dog into their house?

Why not go out and get some malaria and bring it home? Or an anvil? Or a tornado?

The dog was sold to us a 100% genuine Golden Retriever, but by the second day I was having some doubts. I was all set to order up some DNA testing to rule out the possibility the pup's father was a goat, but I can't afford it. My wife just spent my paycheck on fancy dog collars and dog beds and special dog balls and three dozen chewies. And do you realize a small sack of dog chow at Rainbow Ag now goes for $500?!?

And then there's the training. This pup is getting more intensive one-on-one training and tutoring than my two kids ever got in all their years at Ukiah High.

The dog (her name is Katrina in case you find a lost dog with that name on her collar and want to collect the $3 reward from me) has a woman named Sallie coming over a hundred times a week in the hopes of instilling wisdom and virtue and table manners into the pooch. It might be working: the dog has already taught me to take her on walks and feed her on schedule.

But as with any dog, Katrina's main job is determining her position in the family pack. It's fairly easy because my wife, Teri, is the one who hugs her and squeezes her and coos in her ear. I'm the one who forgets her name and forgets to feed her and forgets I left her in the car when I stop at Vic's Tavern for a few quick ones.

And then there's the cat.

Our cat is 12 years old and is a bit set in his ways. He's shaped like a soccer ball with a softball glued on top for a head. He is grouchy and touchy and resentful. He doesn't like the newcomer. The cat is the biggest obstacle to happiness in the young dog's life.

So every morning the pup wakes up wondering if today will be different, if today might be the day the cat has a change of heart and is cheerful and playful and willing to wrestle and romp on the living room floor.

And every day the black-hearted cat sneers. *Today is not the day!*

Here is a scene I have witnessed: Kittiboy sits on the big leather chair in the living room and glares at the little dog. Katrina wags her tail hopefully. Her tongue hangs out the side of her mouth.

She gallops off to the corner of the dining room where her smelly blanket is and comes racing back. She drops her squeaky chicken on the rug in front of the cat. It is both a gift and an invitation to play the squeaky chicken game.

Kittiboy is profoundly unmoved.

The dog remains hopeful. She runs back to her blankie and roots around until she finds her grey squeaky toy, the one that looks like an octopus. She brings it back. She drops it on the rug. The cat mutters Satanic curses.

The pup's head snaps back half an inch. She blinks. Then she scampers back to her nest and brings out her prize: the stuffed chipmunk with *two* squeakies inside! It is her favorite tug-of-war toy.

The pup approaches the cat's throne in full submissive mode. She keeps low to the ground but her tail is wagging hopefully, expectantly. She lays the chipmunk down and sits quietly behind it, her eyes fixed on Lord Cat.

And the cat shifts his gaze to the bookcase across the room, ignoring the chipmunk. You can almost taste the contempt he has for the dog. Kittiboy hoists himself off the chair and trundles heavily into the kitchen where he takes up his position at his food bowl. He spends the next 10 minutes noisily grinding away at his crunchies, his back to the scorned puppy.

Score: Cat 1, Dog 0.

Again today.

You and I would be sad and miserable if someone treated us so rudely, especially after we tried to be nice. We might drink too much for a week or consider finding a new home. But that's because we're not puppies.

Puppies are never defeated and never discouraged and never depressed. A puppy therapist would go out of business. Little doggies are happy and cheerful and optimistic and filled to the brim with puppiness.

Katrina is a puppy. She goes to sleep happy. She can't wait for tomorrow and another chance to become best happy friends with her good friend the cat. And maybe, just maybe, the green squeaky frog will do the trick . . . . .

Awards of Dubious Distinction (Cont'd)

Endorsed by the National
Women's Political Caucus

Best Mendocino County Lakefront Beach

Most listened-to program on
radio station KZYX

Tossing out the gift of a lifetime

I have a daughter named Emily who is the sweetest, most thoughtful and charming young woman I know. She is smart, beautiful, courteous, funny and happy. But it was not always so.

Because when she was a child—starting on the day she came home from Ukiah General Hospital in August of 1979, and lasting until she was oh, 22 or so—she was the most willful, stubborn, uncooperative kid I ever knew. It was simply Emily's nature to be defiant and completely immoveable, but with the teeniest of prodding could be far, far worse. Such as if you were to suggest she clean her room.

Now folks, this was at a time when the two of us were living in a small house on North Oak Street and her bedroom could not have been more than 140 square feet. But asking Emily to clean that room was like asking her to straighten up Alex Tsarnas' old junkyard out there on North State Street by the truck stop.

She'd start with planted feet and folded arms—this was an eight-year old, understand—and glare at me. I tried dipping into my bottomless bag of tricks taken from magazine articles with titles like "How to Get Your Child to Help with Family Chores," and made a casual offer: If we finish the room before 2 o'clock we'd go see the new Care Bears movie at the theater. Emily sneered.

"We could get popcorn," I suggested.

"NO!" Emily explained.

So I reminded myself to be patient and that it would be no big deal that Emily's grandparents were coming out from Cleveland on Thursday and might look into her bedroom. The fact that it appeared to be leased to Waste Management Industries wouldn't bother them. Much.

Anyway, Emily and I did not go to the Ukiah Theater that afternoon to see the new Care Bears movie, although since I was not much of a cook in those days we may indeed have had popcorn for dinner. And her bedroom continued to look as if it should have some of that black-and-yellow "Crime Scene Do Not Enter" tape around it.

And dad, frustrated that his cheerful efforts to coax his recalcitrant daughter into helping out around the house had failed, went into his default mode: Subterfuge. I adopted a new strategy. From that point on I decided that if Emily did not want to clean her room, I would clean it myself. Terminal style.

My method of operation was to simply put as many Hefty Bags into play as necessary, using them to transport clutter and debris from her bedroom to the garage. And there those bedroom things would stay, in limbo, unless and until she noticed they were gone. My theory was that if she didn't even realize that the junk from under her bed was missing (a toy, a sweatshirt, whatever) then it must not matter to her. And this way, I thought, I wouldn't have to clean up the same things twice.

So I got to work.

Twenty Years Later

Last Christmas our family was spending a late morning around the living room, the tree glowing softly, the gifts newly opened. We talked of previous holidays and memories. We brought up other years, other Christmas mornings, and I turned to Emily and asked, with genuine curiosity, what her favorite-ever Christmas present was.

"Oh that's easy," came her instant reply, her face beaming that perfect Emily smile. "Best thing I ever got for Christmas was the Sliding Penguins thing that Uncle Pete got me way back when I was a little kid. You wouldn't remember. It must have been at least 20 years ago. Anyway, it was this little battery-operated stairway that these penguins got in line to go up, and then they slid down this curvy ramp and got back in line.

"That thing was so cool," she said wistfully. "I just loved it. I've looked for it a bunch of times over the years but it's gone. I don't know what I did with it."

I don't think Emily noticed my face go blank as I stared back at her. But to this day—as I write this—I can precisely recall the thin bulge those plastic ramps made through the walls of that Hefty Bag as I toted it out to the garage. It sat there for its allotted six months, waiting for her to notice it was no longer in her bedroom.

Emily never knew where that favorite-ever Christmas present went, but when she reads this, she will.

Awards of Dubious Distinction (Cont'd)

First Place, annual Ukiah
Haiku poetry competition

Voted Best Beer brewed in Mendocino County

Let us now honor the pampered pumpkin

Our annual celebration of the big dead useless gourd is upon us, as we find ourselves deep in the heart of Pumpkinfest. It just might be Ukiah's biggest celebration of the year.

This week we honor the great fat largest most huge and bignormous pumpkins we can find, and we tote them to a scale and we marvel at their vast immensity. Which comes to more than half a ton on some of the finest specimens. Most awesome.

These pumpkins are grotesque by any standard you'd like to apply. They are the size of Buicks. All of them are misshapen and most are the color of something a dog in a kennel might huck up after breakfast.

But gather we must for Pumpkinfest, and celebrate we will in the utterly lame fashion that we celebrate things these days: block off School Street, invite a few concession-pushers over from the Central Valley and turn the kids loose on a corn dog or nine. Whee.

And while we gaze, thrilled, at the sheer bloated grossness of these monstrous pumpkins, let us also reflect on a few poignant realities having to do with our harvest season in the real world.

Mendocino County, once a major player in many things agricultural, has mostly lost its way. Older folks remember, as kids, harvesting walnuts and picking hops all along the Russian River from here to Hopland.

Local teens picked prunes for the prune processing plants, and pears were abundant. The county has been home to vast orchards producing cherries, apples and more. Today?

It's all pretty gone. These days not many people would know a hop crop from hip hop. The hops have been turned into grapes and locals are not among those who harvest them.

The vast cherry orchards up at the Butler Ranch off the Boonville Road were bulldozed a decade or more ago, and disappearing along with the trees were all the memories generations of families had of visiting the ranch each spring. There, you could pick as many cherries as you could carry paying Mister Butler whatever modest amount he bothered to charge.

Walnuts? I used to see old Italian men and women bending and stooping around the streets of Ukiah, retrieving walnuts and putting them in sacks, but that was a while ago. Nowadays they just fall from the trees and clutter up the yards and streets and sidewalks. I'll bet 98% of the ones that fell in 2010 went uneaten.

Drive on out East Perkins Street and take a gaze at the future of your local pear industry. The fields have been under siege for years and are losing ground by the acre. To the south the lands that were once home to a million pear trees are now knee-high in a green grassy weedy-looking thing. Could be alfalfa for all I know, or opium poppies. They ain't pears.

Across Perkins Street to the north it looks like a battlefield with the uprooted dead stacked in ugly mounds, a dozen trees to a pile. A few fresh, edible pears still hang from broken branches.

I didn't grow up in Ukiah. I did time in Cleveland however, where something similar has happened in the decades since I've been gone. Back there factories were kings of the landscape. Everywhere you looked or drove or went there were machine shops and warehouses and fabricators.

On top of the heap were the steel mills, mighty fortresses that ringed the southern edges of Cleveland. It was all an interlocked industrial engine that hummed along and brought vast wealth (and, if I understand correctly, a few environmental side effects) to the citizens who lived there.

That was 50 years ago. During the interim you may have gotten the memo advising us that those factories have been shut down and the jobs have disappeared.

There are no precise parallels between the economies of old Cleveland and current Ukiah. Comparisons can never be exact, merely instructive. But jobs are jobs and an economy provides a linked network of wealth and opportunity in a community. A dried-up economy provides little but dusty memories of what's been lost.

Ukiah has indeed lost walnut and cherry and pear trees in past decades. But the elephant in the orchard has emerged and its name is Marijuana. It's possible that local agriculture will reinvent itself once again, and the area will thrive with a homegrown product. All we can do is stand off to the side and watch.

Maybe wine and pot can save the local economy. I really can't imagine that pumpkins are going to do it.

Awards of Dubious Distinction (Cont'd)

Most Popular Dish, Denny's Restaurant

First Place, Yokayo Bowling Alley
Karaoke Night

Senior Moments

Has anyone else grown just the least bit weary of all the coddling we're required to do for old people around here?

It's not enough they get free money just for being elderly. They get their Social Security and pensions and retirement plans and free medical care and half the time disability benefits and Veteran stuff. All that, and they still want the rest of us to volunteer down at the senior center so we can juggle for them or sing karaoke. It's always something.

Meanwhile, how are the oldsters occupying themselves? Well, they lie around in hammocks sipping their gin and Geritol cocktails while teenagers mow the lawns at their estates. After a few hours of Wheel of Fortune on a 19-inch TV they head over to Safeway with a fistful of coupons and ride around on those slow-moving scooter things with tubes up their noses.

They clog up the checkout lines while browsing through their little oval-shaped plastic change container thingies. Gotta find that nickel and two pennies, y'understand.

Can't these old birds get jobs and support themselves and quit being a drain on the hard-working Americans who pay the bills? Of course when you ask one of these benefit sponges about maybe getting a job they always come up with the 41 years at Masonite or the schoolteacher thing or the disability racket they've got going.

And please—no more of this WWII stuff or how you endured the Great Depression. Every generation has to deal with adversity. In my time we had to survive the Disco Era and 45 years of Jerry Brown. Me, I've also had the lifetime yoke of the Cleveland Indians around my neck. Do you see any of us blubbering about a lack of wheelchair access at the county jail? Are we complaining because there aren't enough federal subsidies for hearing aids? Do you hear us whining about no valet parking at the senior center?

And let's talk honestly about that senior center. A bit ageist, isn't it? I mean, where's the middle-aged guy center? I don't even think there's a youth center around Ukiah anymore. Women at least can go hang out at Project Sanctuary, but seniors get the platinum service, believe me.

I'm sure right now you're saying "Well, it's fine and dandy to complain, But why don't you come up with some solutions, Mister Know-it-All?"

You asked for it. Here are suggestions for ways local seniors can help society:

—Visit a branch of your local library and volunteer as a doorstop.

—Go to a police training academy and make yourself available to cadets learning to disarm, disable and take down suspected criminals. Also, laser and taser technologies are changing rapidly, and with your help police can learn the limits of these valuable new law enforcement tools.

—You have a lifetime of wisdom and learning. Put them to use by doing homework for all the kids in your neighborhood. They'll show their gratitude by teaching you and your ancient friends how to reach Level 20 on "Psycho Slayer IV: End of the Universe" on your PlayStation. They'll also download MP3s onto your iPod and Droid, plus help you re-route your wireless apps.

—Speaking of children, obese kids could sure benefit from piggyback rides to school.

—Homeless folks are especially vulnerable during winter months. Why not do your part by compiling lists of cigarette and alcohol needs of those camped under the Talmage Bridge, then making the short fetch to and from The Bottle Shop?

—How about volunteering as a crash test dummy with the National

Teach Your Dog to Shoplift

Highway Safety Administration?

—On a personal note I'd sure appreciate if someone—and why not a senior?—were to come by my house on Monday nights and wheel my big trash and yard waste bins out to the curb. I recently missed part of an inning of a ballgame performing this tedious task. Plus, feel free to keep any recyclable items like plastic bottles or old newspapers! Who says volunteering can't be rewarding?

These are exactly the kinds of things I'm planning to do for others when I get old, although my doctor says that between the crackpipe and the cirrhosis thing I may not get the opportunity.

Life's Simple Pleasures (Cont'd)

Long walks on a secluded beach with that special someone who has remembered to bring a sixpack

The smell of an old dog. Not too old.

Smokin' cigarettes and
watchin' Captain Kangaroo

Wife and I was out huffing paint fumes in the garage a week or so back when all of a sudden from nowhere she decides she's having a vision or idea that she wants to up and leave. Just another of them "I-need-to-up-and-find-myself-on-a-voyage-through-life" kind of experiences she's prone to.

Me, I'm always happy to see her gone, so I stuffed her onto a Greyhound and sent her to her mammy's. Let that old bird take care of the feeding and maintenance for a spell is my opinion.

Now the good news was I got shed of the missus in such a hurry that she neglected to bring along her medication pills, and I have been able to peddle some of the more exotic ones to the poverty-types who gather down to the old Grace Hudson place. Now I'm left to wonder how many times I can reload those particular rare and lucrative drugs with the fellas at the Rite Aid prescription counter.

I peeped at her return ticket which says she makes the incoming bus at 4:20 in the a.m. on the tenth of next month. Gives me a breather and the opportunity to do some free-livin' for a spell. I might even "find myself" if she'll stay missing til about Christmas.

Anyway, while she's gone I kept a little diary, and in slightly edited format it goes like this:

Teach Your Dog to Shoplift

DAY ONE: Trying to plan ahead, so I went over to the Supercuts by Raley's and got me the works: cut, tint, styling, shave, some Old Spice. Chances are pretty fair something will go wrong in the next few weeks and I want to look my best for the Sheriff's booking photo mug shot website.

DAY TWO: Finally think I might have the time to get that old embarrassing tattoo removed, which has kept the wife from ever seeing me naked.

DAY FOUR: Took the dog of hers up to a taxidermist friend out near Comptche who says he has a buyer who collects stuffed Golden Retrievers, plus is willing to provide me another $50 gratis in order to harvest the pup's internal organs. I never knew there was even a market for such. Your sushi is one thing but I personally draw the line at a dog bladder sandwich.

DAY SIX: I quit feeding the cat and already saved enough to buy me a bonus six-pack of Mickey's Malt Liquor. This housekeeping stuff ain't exactly rocket surgery. Plus I can make a pretty good lunch with all those unused cans of cat food.

DAY SEVEN: Haven't flushed downstairs toilet in some time. You reckon them Guinness World Record folks keep track of feats such as this? You suppose the City Council will give me some kind of plaque for water conservation efforts?

DAY NINE: Sold the wife's car, which puts enough extra dough-re-mi into my pockets to make sure none of my girlfriends have to go without gifts during any upcoming holidays and such. Also, found a couple dollars under the front seat before the sale. Was hoping I'd save a bundle by eliminating the automobile insurance too but it turns out I never got none on her car in the first place.

DAY 11: You ever been over to city council-dude Phil Baldwin's place? Ever see that little wood box he keeps out near the fence in order to collect citizen "contributions" to assist him in his efforts to provide good government?

Well, tomorrow I'm supposed to put 20 dollars in plain, unmarked money in that box, and in return, ol' Phil is going to arrange to waive the fees and restrictions and permit requirements for the rattlesnake breeding farm I'm fixing to put in the attic. Already got a gentleman from San Bernardino to rent the space, and he'll be responsible for the venom milking and raising up of the little critters until they're big enough to go to some foster snake home the Hell's Angels run down south It's just one more thing the wife would have put up a fuss about and I don't mean the $20 missing from her purse.

DAY 12: Wife e-mailed, said she met some guy from Chippendale's which as I understand it is a high-end furniture making outfit. Hope he gives her something special to bring home!

DAY 14: Tore up all the orchids and lilies and heritage roses around the place and put in some revenue-enhancing plants, if you know what I mean. Not pot—too obvious. I planted several hundred Afghan poppies instead. Cops could stroll the yard all day and never suspect a thing.

DAY 15: It's Friday which is Sushi Night, so I emptied out the goldfish tank. I find the Angel fish a bit gamey; how about you? I refilled the tank with a nice young Gallo Chardonnay. I'm thinking of taking apart the old Electrolux vacuum cleaner and making a beer bong out of it. Rug never got much of a workout from it anyway.

DAY 19: If you had a sneaky wife who didn't trust you where do you think she'd go hiding her checkbook? Well, mine tucked hers way down into the dirty laundry basket and it took me this long to find it. But perseverance pays off (or in my case it pays off my tab at the Water Trough).

DAY 22: Cat died today, or maybe last week. Gotta make it look like a suicide.

DAY 24: PG&E shut herself down most of a week ago, nights upstairs are getting a mite colder and so I plan to move out into the garage. It should stay right toasty in there if I have all the doors shut tight and keep the engine running on the Plymouth van. Must remember to collect enough siphoned gas from neighbor cars.

DAY 27: She thinks I just lay around drunk when she's gone, but I've already made a rubber band ball, wrote a poem, and put all my warrants

Teach Your Dog to Shoplift

in chronological order.

DAY 30: E-mail from the wife today says she's in touch with some lawyer over whatever's going on with the Chippendale guy, which just shows how dumb she can be. I mean, shipping furniture might require a moving company but it's way overboard to think you're going to need a lawyer. I told you she ain't the sharpest bulb. I'll have a talk with her when she gets home.

Though it now appears she's cancelled her flight or something. She can't do nothing right.

Awards of Dubious Distinction (Cont'd)

Best Hairdo,
Ukiah Valley Cancer Survivor Club

Ukiah's most scenic drive

State Street, that great street

What is it with the streets of Ukiah? Why are there so many weirdos straggling around out there?

From their looks you'd think they were refugees from a carnival sideshow; from their behavior you'd think they were escapees from Pelican Bay.

Drive out State Street in either direction from the center of town and what you'll see stumbling along the sidewalks is human wreckage on a grand scale. Go ahead and check these people out, but I suggest you avoid eye contact.

The first person you see is an angry young man clutching a balled up shirt in his hand, striding aggressively into the intersection, turning his head back and forth, daring anyone to return his stare. I wonder if he's ever done drugs.

Next you spot a woman wearing three coats, a scarf and a hat that looks like it once belonged to an Eskimo. Does she know she's in Ukiah? Does she know that it's August and it's 104 degrees outside? Does she know about this Planet Earth concept?

What about the guy (shirtless, of course) with all the tattoos, holding a leash and dragging around what probably once was a dog? He's talking to himself. Maybe he's reciting the Pledge of Allegiance.

Here's my question: what are all these people so upset about? Why are they so angry? Why are they mad at me? They should be happy. It's a beautiful Tuesday afternoon and apparently their boss has given them the day off. They live in the lovely little town of Ukiah, or at least it would be lovely if we could get rid of all these deranged nutbag losers.

Where are all the normal people? Where are all the folks like you and me and our neighbors? At this point it would be as shocking to see a nicely dressed middle class couple strolling down State Street as it would be to see a pair of polar bears.

Why is our town's main street overrun with dangerous lunatics?

We've all been a few places in our time, but have you seen any other towns taken over by criminals and zombies who wander the streets asking for trouble?

Suppose you were to make your acquaintance with a stranger in, say Boonville or Fort Bragg. There's a fair chance you and your new friend might find yourselves in friendly conversation and perhaps decide to continue your talk over drinks at the bar of a local hotel.

Do you think you could do that in Ukiah? I doubt it, because (a) there is no hotel in Ukiah and (b) the kind of person you would meet on State Street in Ukiah would not be welcome in any bar you'd be willing to enter.

So leave your new Ukiah acquaintance right where you found him. You'll be better off. Keep on truckin' down State Street and in about 20 blocks you'll come across a guy down near Raley's doing back-flips and somersaults while juggling a big plastic sign advertising Caesar's pizza.

And he's the most normal person on State Street.

Golfers to the rescue

Putting together a list of things liberals dislike would be an overwhelming and exhausting task. Liberals don't like most things, especially things that make sense.

Here is a just a teeny-weeny tiny short, quick, incomplete, abbreviated compilation of a few minor things liberals hate:

+ Corporations
+ Technology
+ Big Oil
+ Big Tobacco
+ Big Macs
+ Loggers
+ Banks and bankers and Wall Street and the Dow-Jones and wealth, except wealth accumulated by rock stars, Hollywood celebrities and Al Gore
+ Freeways
+ NASCAR
+ Military anything (except for Cuba and Nicaragua)
+ Golf and golfers and golf courses

Let's talk about that last one. Our progressive friends hate golfers because golfers are rich white guys, not that they say it in those words. It's always masked in a haze of "concerns" about golf courses using too much water or having a big carbon footprint or encroaching on the wild habitat of endangered snails. But we all know that what really bugs them about golf is that it's enjoyed by fat cats driving Cadillacs, right?

Here's the problem: Liberals are also mad crazy in love with things that raise money for worthy projects. Lefties love fundraisers and benefits to increase awareness for this or that. They love events promoting "consciousness" about some silly cause or another.

A couple weeks ago the Ukiah Municipal Golf Course hosted the annual Ron Ledford Tournament, a fundraiser to help rebuild Anton Stadium.

It raised $110,000.

In two days.

The money goes to the reconstruction of a ballpark built 60 years ago by local volunteers, and let's make one thing crystal clear: Not one of the golfers in that tournament will ever personally benefit in any conceivable way from the new ballpark. Not one of them will ever bat cleanup or pitch a shutout or hit the cutoff man or rip a double into the corner.

The money they donated will be spent on kids they don't know and will likely never meet. But it's nice to think that one day some of them might sit up in the stands and watch the kids play a doubleheader at the park they helped restore.

And of course those who donated all this money are routinely demonized by our thoughtful and intellectual liberal neighbors. "They're just a bunch of selfish rich guys who only care about themselves," is how the sneering comments usually go.

Well, OK. Maybe the tournament was full of hedge fund managers and corporate CEOs. Maybe Donald Trump was there. People can think whatever they want.

But I know a few of them, and they're PG&E workers and tile setters and plumbers and appliance salesmen. And when they were done with that tournament on a Sunday afternoon the city had $110,000 for Anton's rebuild that it didn't have on Friday morning.

Let's see the progressives put together a fundraiser that does that. Let's see one of their benefits bring in $110, let alone a thousand times more. Let's see one of their dweeb-feeb bake sales raise enough money to pay for the frosting on a cupcake.

And for once let's have all the liberals who do all the complaining about community support and helping those less fortunate and raising awareness sit down and shut up.

We're sick up to here of all the whining and shouting and accusations that no one cares about anyone except you miserable bunch of lazy cry-babies and do-nothings at the Environment Center and the Democratic Central Committee and the Alliance for this and the Center for that, who are actually only interested in advancing your own narrow agenda and selfish, idiotic programs.

Go raise one hundred ten thousand dollars to benefit all the kids in this entire community—Native American, white, black, Hispanic, girls, boys—and then we'll listen to more of your complaints about how no one ever does anything around here except you.

But until you've got the $110,000, sit down and shut up.

Awards of Dubious Distinction (Cont'd)

Finest Ukiah Valley art gallery

Ukiah noir: I cover the Mean Streets

It was a hot day in the big city and I was heading north on a street called Pine. Minding my own business.

The name's Kramer. I cover this town like ivy covers the Palace Hotel. It's called "Assignment: Ukiah" and it runs straight from the gutter to the bottom of a birdcage. I knock down bigshots. I stand up for stray dogs. I drink alone.

It was Pine Street where I spotted a meter maid scooter half a block ahead. It zagged left across an oncoming lane where no car was coming and parked in front of the pile of bricks the Methodists use when they talk to the sky. The heat made me irritable as Obama at a tea party.

I squinted through the windshield glare as I rolled past the three-wheeler; and speaking of glare the driver shot me one that would have peeled paint.

I gave the look back, but I blinked first. You would've too. She was wearing an outfit that didn't look like any meter maid costume I'd ever seen. It was brown and yellow and four layers of lumpy. She looked like she'd fallen through an awning. Her hat might have been a flower pot, if flower pots had fur trim.

These are the kinds of clues even a journalist can catch, and within a block it hit me: *That was no meter maid!!*

I didn't need a slide rule and a protractor to know things weren't adding up. I figured that with a pencil, a cocktail napkin and a few cold Pabst Blue Ribbons I could puzzle it out. I also knew I could get my entire list of ingredients at the Forest Club. I headed east on Standley Street.

It was hot. Something made me think the meter maid's vehicle was too.

As I approached The Trees I spotted her. If you've been in this line of work as long as I have you know a dame in trouble from six blocks off. She was less than two.

It was a blonde in a white blouse, and her attention wasn't on me. She was mumbling. I heard her say "Last seen at the intersection of School and Perkins Streets."

I gave her the once-over. She had a nameplate and a metal badge. She was on one of those fancy new electric talkers—cell phones they call 'em—that if you ask me don't do anything a phone booth won't. I had her pegged as a cop. A meter maid. I gave her the time of day.

"Missing a rig?" I smirked. She lifted an eyebrow.

I jutted my chin toward Henry Street. "East bound at Oh-900," I said. I did a 360 and headed for The Forest. Those Blue Ribbons weren't going to drink themselves.

By four o'clock I was back at the Daily Journal wearing a groove into the corner of my desk with the rundown heel of my size nine wingtips. I bought myself a drink from the bottle in the desk. My phone lit up; editor calling.

"Heat on two," she purred in my ear. I set fire to a Chesterfield, leaned back and waited for him to bark. I wasn't worried. My warrants weren't going to show, at least not under this name.

"Got a missing parking meter unit. Got you implicated nine different ways, and I ain't started counting on my left hand yet." It was Kaeser. Sean Kaeser.

"Afternoon Sarge," I snarled. "Mind sayin' how ya got me figured for the runaway scooter? And fast forward—I'm on a deadline."

He accused and I denied and after 10 minutes he knew he didn't have enough to get past the DA's office. "So maybe it wasn't you" he hissed. "But you know plenty. Spill."

"I can put a dame in a flower pot helmet in a three-wheeler on Pine. She gave me the ugliest look I've seen since Phil Baldwin flunked his Walmart job interview. Interested?"

Kaeser sighed. "Get down here and sign a statement."

"Reward money?" I asked in the charming falsetto I use on cops. He growled.

"Alright," I said. "But I need one thing before I'll cooperate. Put me in Witness Protection. New ID, new car, new town, new job."

"We can stick you in Covelo with one of those glasses-and-mustache disguises," said the sergeant. "Best I can do."

"No good," I snapped. "You want help putting this broad away? Plant me in Cleveland with a Prius and a job on the Lake Erie wharf."

You could almost hear him blink. There was a long pause followed by a big silence.

I burned more tobacco while I counted holes in the ceiling tile above my head. I stared out the window and watched an MTA bus heave forward. Of course it was empty; it was rush hour. I waited some more. Glaciers moved.

"I ain't hung up yet," Kaeser finally muttered. "I'm listening. But Cleveland? Witness Protection? You want to go to *Cleveland?* Talk to me, scribbler."

"It's the wife," I said. "I'll finally be done with her. She wouldn't go to Cleveland if you gave her a first class Greyhound ticket. And this way I lose the cat too."

"It don't figure," said Kaeser. "It don't make sense."

"I'm a columnist at the Daily Journal," I yawned. "I don't get paid to make sense."

I actually helped crack The Case of the Missing Parking Enforcement Vehicle back in the spring of 2012, and am still waiting for an award from a grateful city council.

Ukiah then and now

At this point I've been living around Ukiah long enough to have seen some changes drift through. In recent decades almost all of them have been for the worse.

I've hammered together a little list of some of the changes I've noticed. You tell me which ones have improved things.

OLD UKIAH HAD:

1. Mom and Pop grocery stores
2. Barber shops
3. Hardware stores
4. The old Carnegie Library was a classic, beautiful building, suitably grand for a temple of learning. It's now a real estate office
5. Locally owned motels
6. Loggers
7. MacNab's Men's Wear

NEW UKIAH HAS:

1. Mom and Pop grow shops
2. Yoga studios
3. Bail bond outlets
4. The new library, built in the '70s is a cheap-looking box that looks like it was made out of parts left over from the old Rite Aid Building
5. Corporate-owned motels
6. Growers
7. MacNab's Men's Wear

8. Masonite property, where hundreds once worked to produce local products from local resources to support local families.

9. Ladies' dress shops

10. Beer joints

11. Pear orchards

12. A city baseball stadium where Safeway now stands.

13. Goat ropers

14. No skate board park

15. City Hall, with a few dozen employees, and all its offices in that two-story building at the corner of S. State and W. Church Streets, to serve a city of 13,000.

16. Fix-it shops

17. Locally-owned restaurants

18. A drive-in movie

19. Todd Grove Park and its old-fashioned one-of-a-kind playground equipment, including tire climbing challenges, tricky wooden bridges, three big tall metal slides, and best of all—The Rocket Ship!!

20. Homemakers

21. Bar fights on weekends among hardworking loggers

22. Teachers

23. Several incarnations of the county courthouse have existed, and each superior to The Big Nasty that squats at State and Perkins today. Walk around it and marvel.

8. The former Masonite factory, over which hundreds squabble, hoping nothing is ever allowed to be built there again.

9. Tattoo parlors

10. Joints

11. Pear Tree Plaza

12. No baseball stadium where Anton Stadium once stood.

13. Dopers

14. No skate board park

15. City Hall, in its splendid mega-complex of tens of thousands of square feet on several acres of property, to serve a city of 15,000.

16. Tarot reading specialists

17. Fast food franchises

18. Video rental stores

19. Today Todd Grove Park has plastic, out-of-the-box play equipment with all the charm of a McDonald's play room. The Rocket Ship is locked, but kids still gaze at it in awe.

20. Meth makers

21. Stabbings on Laws Avenue among punk loser gangstas.

22. Educational professionals

23. The present courthouse is ugly and looks all cobbled together 'cause it was—like gluing a Chevy Vega to a Rolls Royce.

24. Friends and neighbors, and perhaps a local minister, to help you through difficult times.

24. Therapists and counselors to help you through difficult times, then billing you.

There you have it—many decades of "progress" rolled into one handy list. Review it and savor all the fabulous changes your elected officials and public servants have brought right to your home town, at no cost to you. Just kidding about the "no cost" part, ha ha.

Life's Simple Pleasures (Cont'd)

The calm, serene realization the Cleveland Indians will finish the season no higher than third place in the AL Central, which means no anxieties when I open the morning sports section, no sleepless nights worried about the starting rotation, and no particular need to start drinking in the morning shower once the playoffs begin.
Go Tribe! (But not too far)

You are entering a hug-free zone

Fads come and go but I wish one current fad would go away soon and leave me alone forever. I'm talking about hugs.

What makes people think they should be hugging so much? Hugging used to be reserved for rare, appropriate occasions like weddings and graduations and drunk guys trying to see if the babe they're groping is wearing a bra.

But today every time you see someone you're supposed to give them a big old heart-felt embrace. What for? I've got friends I've known 30 years that I've never hugged. Our next hug will be our first and I'll make sure it's our last.

My parents brought me into this world, raised me as best they could, sent me off and later died. I never hugged either one of them the entire run and I doubt it ever occurred to any of us that we should. I've got siblings and as far as I know not one of us have ever hugged another.

But go to some silly event around here—a show at the Playhouse, an art gallery, a restaurant—and you'll have to fight off half a dozen would-be huggers. But hugging is stupid. Hugging among semi-strangers, which is 100 % of the world as far as I'm concerned, is flat-out wrong. It implies a level of intimacy that doesn't exist.

People who are constantly hugging each other must have deficits in their emotional well-being. Why else would they want to turn every encounter into some sort of mini-therapeutic session complete with phony murmurings about how special it is to see someone they just saw last Tuesday?

Why are you and your friends always hugging each other when you meet at the Farmers Market? What's wrong with a nice pleasant "Hello, how are you?" and the offering of an extended right hand to shake? If you need to get extravagant, try clapping your friend on the shoulder, lightly.

Sometimes I think it's only California exhibitionists who indulge themselves in these types of insincere show-off theatrics, but my lovely wife (Italian by birth) insists her family has been hugging everyone but police officers for many generations. She does not expect me to join in this practice and in fact if she caught me hugging her sister she'd assume we're having an affair.

A while back I went to a memorial service at a house out in Talmage and oh my goodness the hugging that went on. You don't always see them coming and one big lady blindsided me with a massive hug complete with warm moist breathings about how wonderful it was to see me.

I wrestled free and gasped my way to the kitchen for a beer. And when I returned that very same lady came rolling at me like a glacier, arms outstretched, ready to swallow me up in another big sweaty hug. Well, two hugs a year is too much for me; two hugs in less than a minute from the same woman is unthinkable. I did a 180 and went out the front door.

A few minutes later everyone else came out the front door too. The house emptied so that everyone could gather around a fire pit for, of all things, a drumming circle!

Wouldn't you know that the very same people who want to hug everything this side of Dick Cheney would also think a fitting funeral finale is a dumb-butt drumming circle? I took another beer from the kitchen, got in my car and drove home, having used up my hug allotment for the next ten years.

What next? When this ridiculous hug mania finally subsides what will take its place? Bend over and sniff each other's rear ends?

Von's Rock Shop, the living fossil

I recently went somewhere we've all been, although none of us have been to it in many years: Von's Rock Shop.

Yes, Von's Rock Shop, that musty, dusty, cluttered old souvenir stand on Highway 101 a few miles south of Hopland, a place that time and the freeway long ago passed by, is still standing. In fact it appears to be standing still, like it's 1960 or something. That's a sweet thing.

The floor is so worn away the next layer is going to be dirt. The ceiling is falling down because of decades of rain and sun and gravity. The windows are almost opaque but anything else would seem incongruous in a building that houses Von's Rock Shop.

Besides, four walls do not an institution make, and Von's, in its own modest Mendo-way, is an institution. I don't know how long Von's has been in operation, but I certainly can't remember a time when it wasn't there. Yet it doesn't take a lot of imagination to realize the time might come that it isn't.

Most places like Von's have long-since disappeared from the national landscape over the past half-century, but it used to be that you'd encounter any number of oddball stands in the course of a cross-country drive. There were always places that sold "genuine" Indian blankets and maps to nearby silver mines, shops that housed and displayed reptile gardens and prairie dog farms, plus stuffed armadillos for sale in the lobby.

Those places are gone now, as gone as Route 66 or the sand-covered two-lane roads my family used to drive on vacation trips to northern Michigan, where we'd stop at stands selling copies of the Constitution alongside bullwhips with snakeskin handles, and homemade paper tubes containing peanuts with a prize inside. All are gone, along with the home-made birdhouses for sale and the meat-and-potato pastie stands.

Yet Von's Rock Shop is still standing, although now it's a hundred yards east of the 101 freeway that once nourished it with a steady stream of tourists. Today Von's is its own destination point, complete with an on- and off-ramp (and my guess is it's the least-used off-ramp in the entire state of California).

But head into the spacious parking area (sorry, valet parking is unavailable at Von's Rock Shop). I took a spot next to the front door and strolled on in like it was 1983, which may have been the last time I actually visited. The proprietors of Von's, knowing that I like continuity and am skeptical of so-called "progress," have kept things pretty much the same as they were 27 years ago.

Inside Von's Rock Shop are rocks. There are racks and stacks and bins and boxes of rocks and rock-like related items. There are fossils over here and dinosaur bone fragments over there. There are outer space rock chunks and small stones that look pretty much like the gravel in your neighbor's driveway. There are all kinds of polished rock slabs that look like great big jewels. Small jewels too; in fact there's something for every budget at Von's.

While I was there a pair of young girls roamed the shop, carefully picking through the rock displays before finally stepping to the counter. The semi-gruff proprietor carefully toted up the prices, which came to more than $20, and advised the young ladies they owed him precisely $15. The girls exchanged guilty glances, protested half-heartedly that he was charging too little, and then hurried out to the car where mom, in sunglasses, sat waiting in the SUV.

But it's not just the rocks and the prices that will capture your heart at Von's, it's also the melancholy Christmas décor that pervades the place. The silvery, tinsel-style strands that hang from one upright post to another have probably drooped there since the 1970s, given the state of their sagging, dusty despair. Several red ornaments, coated in dust like everything else, hang from the strands

All around the store are magazines of the "Today's Rocks and Gems" type strewn about. I didn't check any dates but I wouldn't be surprised to find issues from before you graduated from high school. There are cardboard boxes and old soda cartons stacked behind the counter. If a fire marshal walked in he'd call for back-up.

My visit to Von's Rock Shop was one of the happiest half hours I've spent in many months. Go on down and bring a few bucks with you. Better yet, bring a few kids.

Awards of Dubious Distinction (Cont'd)

Annual Fred Astaire Choreography Award,
SPACE Dance Academy

Valedictorian, South Valley High School

Voted Best Downtown Mural

Music box Church bells

About 30 years ago the old iron bells at the Ukiah Methodist Church went silent and there was soon a call for contributions to fix them. I was a nearby neighbor so I sent in $25, which as it turned out was $25 I could have spent on more crack cocaine.

What a waste!

Don't get me wrong—I love church bells, At times solemn, at times majestic or melancholy or triumphant, there is something rich and evocative in the clanging, banging resonance of church bells. The pealing of a church bell can lift my spirits or bring a tear to my eye. Church bells sound grave, profound, important and timeless.

And as anyone who lives within a mile of the Ukiah Methodist Church knows, that's not at all what the present-day "bells" sound like. The old bells—with the help of my $25—were replaced with some cheap cassette tape system that plays jaunty tunes that sound like they're coming from Minnie Mouse's music box.

The church now plays a sweet, synthetic rinky-tink concoction of xylophone music done in pastels. It's busy, fake and irritating as it can be, especially from my house, which is only a couple blocks away. You can squeeze your eyes shut and clamp your hands over your ears, but the artificial music still seeps in and forces you to start drinking even though it's only 10 o'clock in the morning. Again today!!

I'm sorry, but these bells don't ring or clang or do anything similar to what traditionally came from church towers. The Ukiah Methodist Church sound machine instead exudes pop tunes that manage to be both sugary and cheesy at the same time. It's a deadly combo that has wearied me for decades.

Many times a day, seven days a week, I get grandiose cotton candy churchbell-style versions of 1970s Top 40 tunes like "Morning has Broken" by Mooslah Foobish (AKA Cat Stevens) or "Michael Row the Boat Ashore," which was an old hootenanny favorite from when your parents were teens.

So I'm plagued by the bells, the swirling and the twirling of the bells. The cloying and annoying, the clinky and the tinky and the manufactured wind-up toy calliope sound of the bells bells bells. Shall I laugh or weep?

So I sit on my front porch and I open another beer and console myself because it certainly could be worse. I could be listening to KZYX, for instance.

Zen of Dog: Drop leash, learn lesson

It wasn't exactly that I was tired of my dog, it was just that I was tired of all the hassles involved in walking her.

It got to where I hated taking her on walks because she refused to behave. Whenever I put the leash on her she'd act like she'd just had a great big snort of crack cocaine and would start jumping around and running in circles and doing cartwheels.

Then when she got on the sidewalk she'd lunge at every leaf blowing by and if she saw a gum wrapper she'd do everything in her power to strangle herself to death getting at it. A cat spotted two blocks away transformed her into a 60-lb frenzy of barking yellow fur.

Over the last year I'd grown weary of the nonstop yanking and pulling that she does on every single block around town. What's the point? My shoulders were sore from getting dislocated three times a week and I was tired of having to apologize for her jumping on everyone we met, including people with crutches and wheelchairs. Who wants to walk a dog like mine?

Last summer the darling wife was out of town for a couple months and on my daily Things To Do list was the dog-walking chore. Dutifully I'd strap Katrina into her pink leash-and-collar apparatus, step out onto the front porch and immediately get pulled eight feet through the air as she leapt off the porch onto the sidewalk. Let the walk begin!

One day we were on our usual route through deepest darkest west side Ukiah. We went up Standley Street and over to Barnes, right on Clay and up to Highland Avenue. When you go left on Highland you're on a long steep hill. I was about a quarter of the way up that hill, shoulder aching from dog yanks, when I had an idea.

I dropped the stupid dog's leash. Just let go and left it for her to drag behind.

I figured there wasn't much chance she'd do anything too dangerous given that it's a rather remote stretch, and that if she felt like pitching herself over the cliff on my left, so be it. Die in an overgrown patch of poison oak off the side of a mountain, you crazy hound!

Plus, if all went wrong I still had almost three full weeks to come up with a plausible lie to tell Teri about where her dog went.

But the dog went nowhere. She trotted alongside me as well as she did when I had a death-grip on her leash. We got over the hill, back to civilization, I picked the leash up and we resumed the walk.

The next day we retraced the route and again when we hit Highland I let go of the pink leash. She poked alongside as if she knew what she was doing, occasionally pausing to sniff a phone pole, once in a while inspecting a cigarette butt, but overall she stayed within a few feet.

We got around to the bottom of the hill and I just let the leash drag. Twenty minutes later we were home. She never drifted more than 10 feet from my side. There were times we saw other dogs and some kids but didn't seem much interested. How did this happen?

My dog had been the most ill-behaved canine any of my friends had ever known and suddenly she's a role model? Suddenly I'm every dog owner's envy? Suddenly they want me on the cover of Dog Lover Monthly?

I'm not sure what happened and I'm not sure it will last. Therefore I'm going to do what anyone else would do, which is to try cashing in quickly and making as much money as I can.

Is your dog's behavior less than perfect? Do you want to be admired by all your pet-owning friends? Would you like your dog to conduct himself in public as if he were on Valium?

Call me. I'll arrange for a somewhat low-cost consultation to determine if your dog might benefit from the TWK Training System. See if my intensive six-week session won't enable your dog to gain new obedience skills along with a healthy respect for authority.

Teach Your Dog to Shoplift

How an education can really pay off

I've been through various graduation exercises and am familiar with the assorted feelings they evoke. There is inevitably a sense of accomplishment mingled with relief, plus pride and exhaustion, whether you're the graduating kid or the parents in the audience.

And that's how it was a while back when I attended Lucas' commencement ordeal up in Canada. It was fine, it was great, and thank God pretty soon it was over. There were the usual pointless speeches about how an education is important in today's world, and how every student's future was limitless, provided he or she worked hard. I didn't feel the need to take notes.

All things considered I suppose the University of Victoria put on a pretty good show. But it was really nothing compared to my all-time favorite graduation scenario.

It was a beaut, and it took some planning.

The best-ever graduation celebration took place when Lucas got out of Pomolita Middle School around 2003 or so. We decided it would be a perfect opportunity for merriment at someone else's expense. The "someone else" was going to be darling daughter Emily, who at the time was in her early 20s.

Emily had also graduated from Pomolita a number of years earlier and she thus understood the approximate value we placed on graduating from middle school. I think we took her to dinner at the China Chef and gave her a $15 gift certificate to the Mendocino Book Company. She would never suspect our treachery.

I called family members and enlisted friends and it was all set up in advance. We had a barbecue the night after graduation and invited a few people over, purportedly to help celebrate young Lucas' fine achievement.

Dinner was served and then it was time for The Main Event: A handful of greeting cards sent from family members and friends were about to be opened, heh heh heh.

Have I mentioned that Lucas was in on the prank? Well, he was and he took fiendish delight in carrying it out. He gobbled down the cake, he expressed modest thanks for the $15 gift certificate from the Mendocino Book Company. Then he got down to business.

The first card was from my brother, a droll and taciturn fellow not given to untoward excitability; my kids know him as Uncle Bill. Lucas read the card's sentiment aloud, and then noticed there was a check enclosed.

"How much?" someone asked innocently.

"Ummm, $500," Lucas replied.

I snuck a peek at Emily, sitting directly across the outdoor table from Lucas. "For graduating from junior high he gets five hundred dollars?!?" she gasped. "Wow! That's great, Luke!"

He then opened a card from Aunt Carol. It too had a check, also in the amount of $500. Emily's eyes popped and her jaw dropped.

"A thousand bucks to get out of Pomolita?!?" she shrieked. "You'd think he just graduated from Harvard!" Lucas just rolled on, opening a card with a check for $1500 from Teri's mother, Grandma Lola, and another, for $500, from good ol' Uncle Pete.

Emily didn't have a calculator and she was having difficulty breathing and so she didn't know what Luke's running total was, but she understood it was well north of $3000 by now.

"Is everybody in the world crazy?" she gasped. "This is eighth grade. People act like he just cured cancer. Am I on the wrong planet?"

No Emily dear, just the wrong family. You certainly deserve better.

By now our neighbors, Kevin and Danna, were handing Lucas their card, and Lucas gleefully tore it open, read the cheap "ConGRADulations!" rubbish and passed around a Wells-Fargo check, signed by Danna, for $5000. At this point Kevin patted Lucas on the elbow and quietly advised him that an education was important in today's world, and that his future was limitless provided he worked hard.

I looked at Emily. She didn't blink for at least 60 seconds and then she put her head back woozily and closed her eyes. She looked exhausted and defeated.

An hour or so later we told her the whole thing had been staged. We tore up all the bogus checks.

I wonder if Emily lay awake that night wondering how all this came to pass and, given all the billions of families on the planet, why she had to be born into mine. I wonder if Lucas ever doubted the wisdom of helping put on such a preposterous stunt simply to make his sister doubt her sanity.

I wonder if I should have re-examined my parenting techniques and instead of devoting my energies to elaborate hoaxes involving my kids had maybe spent more time at places like Disneyland and Tahoe.

Well friends, I just re-read that last paragraph. I've decided everything I did was actually fine and that I taught my kids lots of valuable lessons in life.

And one of these days I suppose they'll teach me a few back.

Hurry up and wait

Wherever I go around town I'm always standing in line, and it doesn't appear that there's ever much reason.

I go to Safeway and it takes me about six minutes to zip through the aisles and get the goods. Then it takes about six hours to get through the checkout line. The line is full of dimwits pushing carts. The wait is always lengthy and always painful.

It usually goes pretty much like this: the woman ahead of you has about 14 items, so you do the quick calculation and estimate she'll be done in a few minutes. It is a gross miscalculation, and I've made it so many times I think I need a new abacus.

The woman starts putting her stuff on the conveyor. Then she:

+ Diddles her number three different times into the Club Card discount pad before she gets it right. She doesn't know her own phone number?
+ Asks about some stupid Buy One, Get One Free items that the nice cashier carefully explains to her a dozen times.
+ After the total is rung up she discovers some coupons in her purse. They expired two weeks ago, but that doesn't prevent several minutes of lively discussion.
+ The cashier says "That'll be $35.17 please" and the woman suddenly

realizes she has to pay. No kidding—it comes as a big surprise. She fumbles with her purse and then she fumbles with her checkbook and then she can't find a pen and then asks what the total is again.

+ And then she decides to use a credit card. No, wait—maybe a debit card. Which one is which?

Then she wants to talk about those coupons some more.

I had come to Safeway to get some hot dogs for a summer BBQ, but as I stand in line I see the clerks and stockboys are starting to put up Christmas decorations. The milk in my cart has gone sour. I look outside and it's raining. Tears roll down my cheeks.

But at least at Safeway or Raley's I can figure out what's taking so long, sort of. It's the debit card thing or it's the no-foodstamps-for-tequila thing or some other semi-comprehensible delay. But why do things move so slow at Bank of America?

I stand at the little table waiting my turn. There's a guy at the counter who was there when I walked in and he'll still be there when I walk out. What is he doing? His income taxes? Is he applying for a job as vice president at the Ukiah Bank of America branch? Is he asking the teller for a date? (Note: I have been on entire dates—the dinner, the drinks, the waking up the next morning—that didn't take as long as this guy is taking to complete some banking transaction.)

And it's not much better at the ATM. I drove up a while ago as I was listening to the A's game on the radio. I parked and walked over to the ATM, and by the time I got done waiting in line and then attending to my 45 seconds at the kiosk the Tigers had batted around. What is it that other people do at ATMs that takes so long? Are they downloading music? Are they filing for bankruptcy?

Or the Ukiah Theater. Why the delays in the line there? What is the doofus in the Hawaiian shirt doing at the ticket counter that takes eight minutes? Is he asking for reviews of each movie from the kid selling tickets? Does he want to know who the gaffer was in "Batman Returns"? Does he need directions to Lakeport?

If the guy takes much longer I'm going to miss the first 20 minutes of commercials that the Ukiah Theater makes you sit through before starting the movie that was supposed to begin at 7:15.

I don't go to fast food joints so that I don't experience the exquisite torture of standing in line at, say, Taco Bell, while the guy in front of me orders stuff off the Burger King menu.

Then there's the DMV, the place for people who love to wait go to wait. It's the Lexus of waiting corrals. It's got plenty of uncomfortable plastic chairs to not sit in and lots of cool posters to memorize. A couple hours studying "Use Your Seat Belt" and "Don't Drink & Drive" always helps me feel inspired, educated, and a better citizen.

Then I go home, having spent the entire day waiting in various lines around Ukiah. But since I've been to the ATM at least I've got a pocketful of cash. So I announce to my latest wife when I come through the door that we should go out for dinner and drinks.

"Oh great!" she says excitedly. "I'll put on some makeup. It'll just take a minute."

That was at 5:30. The Broiler closed at 10 o'clock. We missed it.

Awards of Dubious Distinction (Cont'd)

Best homeless camping spot on railroad tracks

Ukiah area newspaper Columnist of the Year

Art censors keep one eye closed

For a clue as to what makes Ukiah so squalid and forlorn just take a few minutes to drive around town and look at the murals. Be sure to look at them all.

Right downtown we have a collection of terrible murals produced by unskilled children and erected via the aid, comfort and grant money of the local arts and education bureaucracies.

Meanwhile, out on North State Street we have a series of six new murals gracing the exterior of Pacific Outfitters. The differences between these and the grant money murals are stark and informative.

Why is it that the artwork endorsed and supported by the arts community is so ugly?

What is it about educators, teachers, artists, consultants, government agencies and grants writers that conspire to produce such hideous messes? And why do they inflict the ugly junk on us? Why do we have to endure the blight of these monstrous artworks simply because some talentless and unschooled child had a hand in painting them?

Every mural produced within the past 15 years that is now hanging in the downtown area is an insult to the public and an affront to any reasonable aesthetic sense.

These creations violate each and every known principle of art, whether in composition, color scheme, perspective or subject matter. Local citizens suffer doubly. We are required to subsidize this depressing rubbish and then we're forced to look at it on a daily basis.

Contrast the murals produced under the guidance and mentoring of government agents to the obstacles a local business faces. Instead of getting assistance and applause at every step of the way, a store owner has to negotiate a labyrinth of government hurdles in order to legally place six measly paintings on the outside of a shop.

Just imagine the obstructions and delays cheerfully thrown in the path of someone trying to get something done in Ukiah. The regulations—licenses, fees, codes, health requirements and environmental demands—would be enough to make anyone give up trying to build a factory. But to hang a few paintings?

Because after first surviving the bewildering array of business restrictions, next come the Planning Commission overlords. These are the snobbish, politically correct busybody zealots who believe forcing others to bend to their naïve political views and stupid artistic whims is the essence of the job

When the proposed Pacific Outfitter artwork was submitted to Planning Commissioners, the response was as follows: "You'll have to change it! There are too many white males in that scene!"

The response to the next painting was "No no, change it! There's a hunting rifle visible!" Changes were demanded. Changes were made. Government censors prevailed.

But where is the government review team to insist that the garbage coughed up at Rural Murals adheres to acceptable standards of content? Who guarantees that murals depicting farmers and shopkeepers are in numbers corresponding to their population, at least in comparison with the numbers of reggae musicians, gurus, unicorns and earth mamas on display?

Where are the diversity police when it comes to the downtown murals? Why do the enforcement regulators only monitor small businesses for perceived lapses in artistic correctness? Why doesn't the Planning Commission bully the perpetrators of that big, grotesque mosaic at State and Perkins Streets for failing to include sufficient numbers of men driving pickup trucks?

Because the Planning Commission doesn't like men driving trucks, that's why. Or hunting rifles. Those images fail to please the commissioners.

The Ukiah Planning Commission is a government agency full of unelected bureaucrats that demand citizens adhere to their theories of appropriate standards *or else.*

Or else permits will be denied. Or else inspectors will visit and review boards will meet. Memos will be written. Lawyers will be consulted. Certified letters will be sent. Threats will be made. Fines will be levied. Penalties will increase. Or else we will not allow you to open your building.

But please remember: The City of Ukiah looks forward to working with you in a positive manner. Together we can build a strong and vibrant business community.

Life's Simple Pleasures (Cont'd)

The happy, chirpy sounds from the ice cream truck
rolling around the west side are a delight. For 15 minutes.
After that I feel like "Home, Home on the Range" is
being subliminally planted in my brain and I'll be
hearing it in 3 am. nightmares for the rest of my life

All those vacations that I try to avoid

I'm leaving soon for a few weeks off
I'll be missing my friends at the Water Trough
Might wind up in London or the jungles of Maya
But wherever I go it just won't be Ukiah
I weep as I think of a day spent away
From the coolest best place in the whole USA

Now some folks might like a luxury cruise
But where would I score my meth and my booze?
Some say a great vacation is a five-star hotel
But to me that sounds like three weeks in hell
Waiters and servants and long quiet halls?
The only thing worse might be vacations in malls

I prefer strolling State Street without any cares
Dragging my pitbull down to Plowshares
Or meeting my mates at Grace Hudson Park
We drink 'til we drop, or until it gets dark
Then on to the railroad tracks, a party each night
You can always find drugs, and sometimes a fight

(CHORUS):
A new day is dawning, I see sun coming in
Through the bottom of a bottle of Raley's brand gin
In the Walmart parking lot, where I woke up again

I'm sure Tahoe's nice, like the grand Biltmore grounds
But why miss a Tractor Pull at the local Fairgrounds?
Demolition Derby? Monster Truck competition?
I wouldn't trade either for Florida fishin'
Ladies' Night at the Forest Club, drinks are half-price
I have to wear a wig (but I look pretty nice)

Don't want gay Paree, where they eat snails and slop
I prefer liver and onions out at Jensen's Truck Stop
A corn dog at the county fair is plenty good for me
No need for a snooty hotel's four o'clock tea
Just give me a sixpack and a beef jerky stick
As I roll around town in my silver Crown Vic

So a vacation sounds swell until I leave town
And realize I've left the best place around
Where bikers and trimmers and other illegals
Roam through Ukiah like a dump full of seagulls
The downtown's crumbling, we're shutting it down
But our homeless services are the finest around!

(CHORUS):
A new day is dawning, I see sun coming in
Through the bottom of a bottle of Raley's brand gin
In the Walmart parking lot, where I woke up again

I hear people say that there's no culture here
What about Pumpkinfest and Blue Ribbon beer?
Our murals and sidewalk chalk art are a delight
Go have a look for yourself (but not in daylight)
We have Sunday Concerts where old hippies dance
It's easy to join 'em—just take off your pants!

I always regret it when I drive 101
I wish my trip was over before it's begun
Rolling up Burke Hill just fills me with fear
I dread seeing Ukiah in my rearview mirror
The mayor might do something I'd sure hate to miss
Like exposing her butt for the vice-mayor to kiss

So I'd rather stay home, where my heart's always been
I'd rather not travel and miss friends and kin
So I think I'll cancel reservations today
For the trips I've planned to Dubai and LA
I'll just stay in my house and tuck myself in
And for a treat I'll switch to Safeway brand gin

Teach Your Dog to Shoplift

Think of all you've done with your life!

You're getting old. Every day you scan the obituaries and get that anxious, sinking feeling when you see that, again today, all the dead people listed in the newspaper are younger than you. Years roll by like months once did. Christmas seems to come four times a year.

You're getting old and you know it. Mostly you shrug it off, but there's a hollow feeling at your core, a gnawing suspicion that maybe you've made some critical mistakes. Perhaps you bet too heavily on the '60s generation and the youth culture and that Hope-I- Die-Before-I-Get-Old mantra. Because now you realize that you've already gotten old, and pretty soon you're also gonna die. Lots of people younger than you already have.

What will you have to show for it? Everything you've accomplished in the past few decades suddenly seems rather . . . watery. You have the panicky feeling that maybe your life peaked when you saw the Rolling Stones at Candlestick in 1985.

I have good news. Quit worrying. You've done great things with your life, but of course you don't like to brag about it. That's just you. Yet you've accomplished so much. You've truly made the world a better place.

Let me review some of the more noteworthy things you've already done in your lifetime:

1. You read "Walden" by Henry David Thoreau three times one summer.
2. Because you always cared about the needs of others, you were once on the board of directors at the Ukiah Community Center, at least until there was a scheduling conflict with Monday Night Football.
3. You would like to be made part of one of those Oral History projects due to your penetrating insights into the decades-old controversy surrounding Paul McCartney. Is he dead? Was he the walrus? You have some intriguing theories.
4. By the time you were 19 you already knew pretty much everything about culture and politics and thus were able to glide through the next half-century without ever needing to re-examine any of your opinions or beliefs.
5. You were the first person in your dorm to wear granny glasses and Frye boots.
6. You married your first wife based on astrological compatibility, as you were told that she, a Gemini, was particularly attracted to your Taurus (with Jupiter rising). Your astrologer said you were Soul Mates. But it turned out your wife was even more attracted to Sagittarius men. And some Pisces women. Which was cool.
7. You were the first student at your college to write a term paper about Star Trek.
8. If you're female you struck proud blows against sexism and gender inequality by screaming feminist slogans at your father (now deceased) your grandfather (deceased) and your two uncles who haven't spoken to you since 1978.
9. If you're male you joined a drumming circle.
10. You donated to worthy causes all your life. You gave generously to the Sandinistas, Huey Newton's defense fund, and all six of Dennis Kucinich's Presidential campaigns.
11. You know every word to every song on the "Abbey Road" album.
12. All your friends know how much you love children, and that you once volunteered for an afternoon at the annual Caring Community Children's Fair Day.
13. It was always important to you to experience other cultures in

order to gain empathy and understanding of indigenous people around the world. These convictions, (along with unreliable bus service) resulted in your once spending three days in a somewhat remote Mexican village. It exposed you to their simple yet charming poverty. You tell everyone that you made a lifelong connection with them.

14. Although you have long insisted that foreign films are vastly superior to the fluff churned out in the USA, you also recognize Hollywood as a powerful, positive tool for political and ideological progress both here and throughout the world.

15. In 1974 you had the Zig-Zag Man tattooed on your right bicep. In 1986 you had "Question Authority" tattooed on your left shoulder. In 2008 you had "Hope & Change!" tattooed across your chest. These powerful images demonstrate the evolution of your social awareness and consciousness.

16. When you die (or, rather, pass into a dimension other than this) you want Tibetan Mountain Flute Music played at your funeral (or, rather, the "Celebration of Life" held in your memory). Of course the music doesn't have to be played by actual Tibetans, because you don't know any. You also don't know where Tibet is, exactly.

If it's too much of a hassle, your brother has a bootleg cassette of The Grateful Dead jamming with the Allman Brothers. That would be fine too.

You say 'Haiku' and I say 'Gesundheit'

Whoever invented Ukiah probably also came up with the Haiku festival, held here once a year and a very big deal because Ukiah is Haiku spelled backwards. If that's not a big deal, what is?

So once a year word goes out to poets all over the land to submit haiku poetry for the annual contest in Ukiah. And these poets—some from as far away as Kelseyville, send in their favorites samples of the ancient art.

Haiku poetry is entry level Japanese verse that could be mastered by a six year old on her second try. Here it is: three lines, the first and last of which contain five syllables. The second line has seven syllables. Got it? That wasn't so hard, right?

So the entries come in, like I say, and since this is Mendocino County our local poets and artists and other sensitive sorts compose their best haikus on top quality (recycled) paper in lovely lavender ink. They all go like this:

My soul yearns, blossoms
Like petals upon the wind
Through my empty mind

Did you get the five-seven-five syllable thingie? Here's another typical of what will come to the festival's judges:

Caring and sharing
My soul and spirit transcend
A world that's within

You get the idea: all dwibbery jibbery holistic goo. Those entries into the UkiaHaiku festival give you absolutely zero insight into reality around here. And if a poem can't illuminate our lives and give meaning to our surroundings, what use is it?

Here are haikus that actually reflect our place and our time:

Dead dog in blue car
One-oh-six in August shade
Man Ukiah's hot!

Former friend outlawed
Banned, hated, driven from town
A plastic bag's fate

Money for nothing
Oh to be a consultant
Here in Ukiah

Wife left and dog died
My unemployment ran out
Hello, Forest Club!

Haikus are easy
But sometimes they make no sense
Lake Mendocino

Brain fever, cancer
Hateful corporate poison
Smart Meters are here

Homeless with backpacks
Pit bulls, bums and sleeping bags
State Street, that great street!

Ukiah nightlife:
_____,
_____ and _____

Forgotten people
Nursing homes on South Dora
Old folks' warehouse

Limo's to dog parks
Steak dinners for our canines
Next: Dog for Mayor

Our town: Nine miles long
And one block wide, all ugly
The tourists drive by

Crystal energy
Rainbow warrior for peace
Guess what? I smoke pot

Grant money is free
Which is why no one ever
Has to work for it

Your job stinks, but think
You could be a realtor
And suicidal

Boozers on the tracks
Losers at the city parks
You and me stay home

Teach Your Dog to Shoplift

Ukiah is great
We're so lucky to live here
We lie to ourselves

Medicine spirit
I got my 215 card
Oh look, watch me heal!

Fuzzy know-it-alls
Boring prattle of yoga
Our Farmer's Market

Puppies and kittens
Up for adoption will make
A fine Plowshares lunch

Woodstock Nation: Groovy Generation

Woodstock came and went 40 years ago, and we simply must have faith that all the current anniversary blahzoo will also soon fade into the dustbin of nothingness where it belongs.

"Celebrating" Woodstock is the perfect story for today's media as it fawns over dried-up Boomer celebrities after first marinating them in a stew of supposed historical significance. It's a modern "news" story presented by the journalistic feebs who formerly produced actual news. Writing about the Meaning of Woodstock gives them respite from their chores covering Paris Hilton.

Did you know I was at Woodstock? Well I was, squirming in the muck just like all the other rodents at a barn dance. In recent years I've come to think I ought to apologize to someone but it's too late for my parents, who stumbled to early graves no doubt suspecting their middle son was still a loser bum. And I was.

But now I'm not. Now I'm a cheerful right-thinking chap who sees Woodstock as the nightmare event that kick-started our downward spiral into the bottomless sludgepit of social decay. Which is where we find ourselves today, trapped in a Baby Boomer culture that thinks the Universe was created in order to provide entertainment and amusement for it.

Woodstock was supposed to get us back to the land or back to the garden, or maybe it was going to change the world. It did none of these things, and in fact all Woodstock changed were the income levels for electric guitar players and bad songwriters. Since August, 1969, rock performers have been considered stars and gods and heroes. They are worshiped and idolized as visionaries and saviors. Also, they are all trillionaires.

How do you like your Baby Boomer values so far?

And how do we explain someone like Jackson Browne, a quiet, whiney sort of rocker, being recognized across the land as a high authority on all things environmental? What about Bono? He's an international player on the world stage, on equal footing with Condaleeza Rice and Bill Clinton, simply and only because he recorded some pretentious twaddle 20 years ago about teenage sharing and caring.

Woodstock elevated cheap pop celebrity status over actual achievement and the world's been worse ever since. I don't remember anyone consulting Ricky Nelson or the Shangrilas or Chuck Berry on the gripping social and political questions of their day.

The Love Generation believes it is the greatest generation and that Woodstock is the greatest celebration of its shining glory. There is no sense to any of this of course, but brace yourself because it looks like the media will continue chewing its Woodstock cud until it can find another Michael Jackson death or Bruce Springsteen lobotomy to analyze.

I was at a bookstore on the coast last weekend and saw an entire rack (yes!) of Woodstock-related items. There was a book based on a movie based on a book about Woodstock, and there was even a children's book about Woodstock. Bring back book burnings.

'Frisco's Chronicle had a gushy report the other day by its monumentally silly "Senior Music Critic, Joel Selvin," featuring numerous folks who had been at Woodstock, as if being at Woodstock was on a par with being at Normandy or Nuremberg. But there they were, elderly Boomer dudes trying to look as if they still had their mojo working, with those thin stringy ponytails running down their back like limp tattered banners from a forgotten campaign in a lost war. We were there, baby! Let the world never forget! Oh the Memories!

Well, flush those memories down the sickhole of the failed Woodstock Nation, where childlike innocence and idealism bumped into the cruel realities of ignorance and stupidity. And 40 years later some people still haven't figured out which team won.

Not the best of all possible worlds

We think we are Masters of the Universe.

We think we are on a bright, shiny conveyor belt to the future where endless progress brings limitless advancements to our lives and our society. We think the world will only get better and that the best is indeed yet to come.

How could it not be so? Even without much knowledge or understanding of history we nonetheless all have some tenuous grasp of how bad the days gone by used to be. We've seen the old newsreel footage and photos. The Dark Ages: Dental care was primitive, travel was by horseback, and Pop Tarts only came in strawberry.

But those days are gone and hardly even a memory, which is why the future is going to be so cool. We actually think this.

But the arc of human progress may not be one with a trajectory straight and uninterrupted and destined to bring us a world in which everyone is beautiful and our dog never dies. What guarantee do we have that there is no decline in store for us? Suppose, for example, that an elderly couple from waaay long ago, from back in the distant days of around 1950, could be magically transported by cosmic rays into our time. And also, into our town.

What do you suppose a pair of oldsters from back then (we'll give them names like "grandma" and "grandpa" for easy reference) would think if they were to be plopped down this afternoon on a bench in front of Walmart?

Initially they'd be amazed by our twitters and tweets and the GPS and the MP3s and the SUVs with leather seats. They'd be speechless if handed an iPhone or an iPad, and they'd be impressed with the 42-inch plasma hi-def flat screen TV, and the first black President, and airplanes so fast they land in 'Frisco before they take off from Cleveland.

But soon enough, after all the gaping at the electronic gadgets we show them, grandma and grandpa are going to look around and get an alternate whiff of life in the 21st century. And that's what I'm talking about, folks.

What would your grandparents think when exposed to the boorish, uncouth, foul-mouthed and semi-civilized people we've allowed ourselves to become?

Behold: Obese adult citizens ambling about the streets in plastic flip-flops while wearing flannel pajama bottoms and soiled t-shirts, which at least help hide most of their grotesque tattoos. They grunt loudly into cell phones. Straggling behind is a sullen, obese teenage son wearing baggy denim pants that droop to his thighs. Advising gramps the kid is merely mimicking the way prison inmates dress will probably not reassure him.

Of course not everyone is a chubba waddling about in their underwear. Some drive. They motor around the sidewalks and stores in golf-style carts built for, and given to, fat people. The vehicles are provided by the government to minimize the risk of them burning up too many calories while searching store aisles for tonight's dinner of Doritos, Froot Loops and suet. These are purchased with food stamps. Grandma appears greenish, perhaps with envy.

All the people trudging by are sucking on straws inserted into enormous plastic sippy cups filled with sugary sludge. The cups say "Mega-Belch 64-Oz Free Refills" on the side, and are dropped to the ground when empty.

Also staggering about the sidewalks are mentally ill people talking to themselves and to you. Their families have abandoned them ("She's not our problem!") and the government has abandoned them ("He's not our problems!") but judging from the crazy conversation they're starting with your grandparents, it looks like the nuts will soon be their problem. Maybe granny can hurry up and learn some volunteer skills—very handy in the 21st century!

If gram and gramps get off the bench and wander around town a bit they'll quickly see that every building constructed in the past half-century is ugly, plus is covered with moronic gang graffiti. This will also give the oldsters the opportunity to be assaulted by huge trucks driven by unemployed young men blasting loud, offensive music that will rattle their dentures and cause many nightmares.

The experience as a whole will make your grandparents want to hurry back to 1950, even if they have to leave their Android cell phone with all those free apps behind.

Before they go someone should point out to them that Ukiah was fairly recently named "Best Small Town" in the state of California, and sixth best in the entire USA.

This will make them think the reason they don't fit in with 21st Century Ukiah is their fault.

Things I'll do when I retire

I can already stand on my tiptoes and see the rosy future.

I can see a sunny tomorrow and a better world ahead. Yes, I can definitely see a time when I'm going to retire from my toils in the workforce and start living it up.

Here are the things I'm planning to do when I retire:

1. Change my name to Fabio.
2. Spend more time with my cat.
3. Learn how to twist balloons into funny animal shapes like giraffes and dachshunds.
4. Of course retirement is a time for a husband and wife to become closer to one another. I'm definitely looking forward to that. I can follow her upstairs when she vacuums and show her where she missed a tiny little spot, and later help out in the laundry room by suggesting just a bit more bleach with the wash to help get rid of those crusty yellow stains in all the armpits of my t-shirts. I can even lend a hand in the bathroom. "Open wide," I'll say. "Time to floss!"
5. A few days of this and I can almost guarantee she'll be packing up and driving off.

6. And when she does leave I'll finally be able to invest in a good quality, durable, top-of-the-line inflatable doll.

7. Given the status of my mostly imaginary pension, my Social Security income, and all the wise investments I've made over the years, I'll probably be getting to know the staff at Plowshares pretty well.

8. And if Obama is re-elected I'll be getting to know all the homeless camps along the railroad tracks.

9. I may have to eat my cat.

10. Why didn't someone tell me 30 years ago how much all those aluminum beer cans I threw away would be worth?

11. At last I'll have all the time I want to start hanging out at the Ukiah Men's Yoga Center

12. I should be able to finish writing the Mari Rodin biography I've been working on this past decade.

13. What is it they do down at the Senior Center, anyway? Is there a secret handshake to get in? I know there's free food so I assume there's probably some booze, too, at least out in the parking lot. Plus there are a lot of babes, and they're almost all single. I mean, if what those insurance actuarial tables say is true all their husbands died at 77.3 years. I'll have my pick.

14. Once I quit work I'll be able to really pick up the pace with my production of rubber band balls.

15. Retirement means I'll have enough free time to spend 85 to 100 hours a week helping out and giving advice at the Ukiah Daily Journal, unless K.C. Meadows is serious about that restraining order.

16. When you retire do you get one of those scooter-type things to roll around Safeway for free?

17. I'll be able to go early and stay late at Spring Training. In fact, as bad as the Cleveland Indians have been the past few years I might make the roster.

18. I understand retiring means I'm already awfully old, but I'm definitely looking forward to the benefits: free passes on the MTA buses, half-price movie tickets and senior discounts at Denny's.

Teach Your Dog to Shoplift

19. On the other frail old claw-like hand, does this mean I have to get dentures and start wearing Depends, and take medication with side-effects that include advanced heart palpitations, baldness and exploding thyroids?
20. Think I'll try some of that google stuff I keep hearing about.
21. Attend lots of funerals.
22. And at the last funeral, I'll be the main attraction.

Awards of Dubious Distinction (Cont'd)

Sexiest guy, Mendocino County Jail

Sexiest gal, Mendocino County
Department of Social Services

A fun summer BBQ with dad

A few decades back I was working in an office with a bunch of attorneys and every summer one of them, Kitti Houston, would throw a big party at her house on the south side of town.

It was great. She had a back yard the size of the landing strip at the Ukiah airport, and she had Kevin and Bob and Bo, some of whom were dogs, to help her put it on. Swimming pool, barbecue, and free beer made it mostly tolerable, given the percentage of lawyers generally in attendance.

So one year Kitti announced the date and I circled it on the calendar. A week or two before it happened I decided to see if Emily, daughter dearest herself, would like to come along and frolic away the day. I'm not sure what I was thinking because she was only around eight years old at the time, much too young to be my designated driver. But a father's generosity knows not reason nor limit, doth it?

Emily, being desperate to escape the doldrums of yet another fiendishly hot summer day at our house on North Oak, said she'd go. I suggested she invite a friend along, and she did that too.

On the day of the party I got things ready to go in the morning. I'd made scalding hot salsa from peppers in my garden, I grabbed some bags of chips, put some beer in a cooler and packed it all away in the trunk of my '64 Volvo.

We went over to pick up Marisa Sizemore, Emily's lifelong Best Friend Forever, at her house a few blocks north of ours.

Do you mind terribly if I take a paragraph or so here to tell you just how darn cute and fun and adorable a pair of little girls can be? There they sat in the back seat of the car, happily awaiting a fun day of swimming and splashing. They both had their My Little Pony backpacks and they both had big beach towels (Emily's was blue with a unicorn on it) and they just looked so happy. Sigh.

So away we went. We rolled south on State Street toward Kitti and Kevin's place on Meadowbrook, Marisa and Emily harmoniously humming "Over the Rainbow" in those little girl voices that only angels can rival.

Now dear reader, what followed was not something I'd planned because, after all, how could I? But as we motored along just a little north of the Water Trough bar, I saw a dilapidated, trash strewn parking lot along with a few shabby cabins and a broken maroon-and- white sign that said "Marty's Motel." A light went on in my head. I made a hard right off State Street and I came to a stop about 50 feet from the office. I turned off the engine.

"OK!" I said brightly. "Here we are!" And I grabbed my sunglasses off the dashboard, got out of the car, leaving the door open, and went around to the back and opened the trunk. I carried the ice chest back toward the front of the car. ""Swimming pool is over that way," I said, and made a vague gesture with my chin toward a motel unit at the back corner of the parking lot.

Neither Emily nor Marisa moved, and I don't know if they breathed They sat frozen in the back seat, staring out the windshield at the tableau that presented itself.

There on one knee in front of the closest motel unit was a guy fixing a motorcycle, or at least he was talking to it, angrily. A woman sat leaning forward on an overturned milk crate next to him, smoking a cigarette and wearing a grimy t-shirt that covered her all the way to her knees, which were pushed about 20 inches apart.

Another woman leaned in an open doorway across the lot. She too was smoking and she held a can of beer. Some toddlers, naked except for sagging diapers, staggered around their toy-free playground which was also, of course, a hot, asphalt parking lot.

I remained bright, cheerful and the essence of summer fun: "Come on you two! Get those chips! Grab your towels!"

It would have been the same if I'd invited them to join me in some serpent rasslin' at Big Ed's Rattlesnake Ranch. Emily and Marisa sat wide-eyed, their hands clutching their backpacks. They did not look as if they wanted to go search for the swimming pool.

By now the vibe must have passed through Marty's Motel that some foreigners, *some folks who just don't belong*, had arrived in their midst. Dirty curtains moved and faces appeared through filmy windows. The woman in the doorway flicked her cigarette butt into the parking lot, took a short swallow of beer, and shifted her weight. The motorcycle guy stood up and glared our way.

I'm pretty good at knowing when the best part of a joke has been exhausted and I was thinking that I was maybe 30 seconds past that point. Yesss, I figured, this here Marty Motel caper has gone on just about long enough. I slid the ice chest into the front seat, and I got in and shut the door behind me.

I headed toward the parking lot exit that would dump us back on State Street.

"You kids had enough fun?" I asked. "Ready to go home?"

I made a right turn and, chortling all the way, I headed to the party on Meadowbrook Drive.

HANDBOOK OF
COUNTY PROCEDURES

Thank you for choosing to work for the county! We realize you have many employment options available to you and we are grateful you have chosen us to provide your weekly paychecks.

To help you become acquainted with county policies and regulations, we have compiled the following information. Please take the time to read it carefully.

1. The county work day shall commence at 8 a.m. except on those days and times in which meetings, conferences or seminars are being held, attended, scheduled or planned. In such instances the work day shall commence at 8 a.m. the following day, with the same exceptions for previously noted meetings, conferences and seminars up to, but not including, weekends.

2. Contact with the public is discouraged during normal county office working hours, except for those departments providing services to members of the public bearing checks, money orders, credit cards in payment for county services yet to be performed.

3. Employees are asked to refrain from offering gifts, gratu-

ities, cash or other items of value to their office supervisor or department head in return for promotions, bonus pay or additional vacation time. Such offerings should instead be provided directly to county administrators for inspection and proper disbursement to appropriate recipients.

4. When resting one's heels upon an office desk top please take care to utilize a county-issued rubber mat to protect formica surfaces from excessive wear.

5. The director of county health and wellness services encourages employees to make an effort to stand up at least twice daily, and to move and stretch in the area around your desk. Also, it is recommended that sleep masks be removed at regular intervals throughout the day so that eyes are able to make occasional but necessary adjustments to light.

6. Employees are encouraged to present a clean, well-groomed image when dealing with the public, and basic standards of hygiene and attire are expected. (Note: This provision shall be waived for members of the county's Social Service Department and those employed at the sewage treatment facility).

7. All employees furnished with a county-issued computer shall be provided with a minimum of 48 video gaming devices, including Free Cell, Solitaire, Super Mario II and Warmageddon III: Final Avengers. Also, inspection of pornographic websites shall be limited to the employee lounge areas and / or recognized break times, including lunch and coffee.

8. Employees resting their heads upon office desk tops are encouraged to utilize absorbent mats to prevent unwanted collections of saliva upon formica surfaces. See your department head for six-month supplies of towelettes.

9. Please refrain from smoking marijuana within county offices, except at the beginning of one's work shift, or during recognized break times, including lunch and coffee.

Teach Your Dog to Shoplift

10. All county benefits, including health insurance, pensions and retirement accounts, are managed by county administrators in accordance with actuarial tables based on lunar tide movements and universally accepted horoscope predictions.

Awards of Dubious Distinction (Cont'd)

Laws Avenue Citizen of the Year

Homecoming Queen, Anderson Valley High

Best Dressed member of the Board of Directors,
Mendocino Environmental Center

Drink and drive and cross your fingers

There was a time many years ago when I used to drink and drive. A lot. But so did everybody else I knew, and it did not seem to be a big deal.

It remains a small mystery that I never got a DUI but it certainly wasn't for lack of trying. The cops had a thousand shots at me over the decades. Let me tell you about a couple of close calls.

The first one was my fault, and not because I was stupid enough to drink too much and then start driving. I was down in Sonoma County at some big sweaty event that was alcohol-free. My mistake was that I'd gone to a beer-free event. Like I said, my fault. When the three-hour ordeal was over I staggered to my car and zipped to the nearby Park-N-Drinkit where a kindly clerk sold me a six-pack of Coors in those tiny little 8 oz cans. I drank five in the parking lot in less than two minutes and then I rolled out all refreshed and relaxed.

At least until the red and blue lights filled up my rearview mirror, which unlaxed the hell out of me. I took a deep breath and exited my car (this was back when getting out of your car when pulled over was the polite thing to do; these days a cop will cheerfully install a bullet in your kneecap to remind you to remain inside your vehicle).

"What seems to be the matter, officer?" I asked brightly. Except it wasn't a police officer. The police officer was still in the car. He'd sent out his trainee or his ridealong or some sidekick youngster in a cadet-style uniform to deal with me and my broken taillight.

So we discussed that taillight. I was sucking air all the while and talking out the side of my mouth while backpedaling around the car and helpfully pointing out to him all the numerous vehicle lights that seemed to be functioning quite properly.

I think the trainee was impressed because a minute or two later I was back behind the wheel and a few minutes after that I was seated on a stool at the old (now gone) Melendy's Bar in Santa Rosa, having a beer to celebrate my most excellent good fortune.

That was my first narrow escape.

Then one other time I was working in San Jose and my co-workers and I finished up late on a Friday afternoon and decided to visit a nearby bar and wait for the traffic to thin out before we took our individual routes home. At 6:30 or so I headed up Highway 280 and got off on 19th Avenue on my way through 'Frisco. I stopped at a corner liquor store and got a six-pack of Mickey's Malt Liquor. I rolled north.

By Cloverdale my provisions had been exhausted so I stopped and bought me another sixer of Mickey's and continued my merry way home. On past Squaw Rock I zoomed, but a mile or so later it all came crashing apart. Up ahead was a cop car parked with flashing lights. A uniformed officer was waving traffic over into a single lane.

Oh no. A DUI checkpoint. Oh noooo.

Oh Hollo! Oh frig and frag! What did I ever do to deserve this, I wondered.

I screwed the cap back on my recently opened Mickey's and I slid it under my seat. I rolled down the window and sucked cubic yards of oxygen into my lungs as a cop motioned me over with a flashlight. Oh arrghh!

By now I was going about two miles an hour and I'm promising the saints and the Incan gods and my future probation officer I'll never drink and drive again. Dear Jesus why me?!?

More cops up ahead on both sides of the road as I inch along, flashing lights everywhere on the police cars and the tow trucks and ambulance.

Tow trucks and ambulance?

A light clicks on in my fog-scrambled brain, and off to my right I see an overturned car along with a crushed pickup truck with its hood up. A sheet-covered stretcher is being loaded into an ambulance.

YESSSSS!!

I cannot tell you how happy I was to suddenly realize I wouldn't be getting a DUI, and that all that had happened was there had been a collision and someone who I didn't know got killed.

I reached back under my car seat and fished out the Mickey's. I unscrewed the cap and drank to my most excellent good fortune.

Life's Simple Pleasures (Cont'd)

Driving down State Street and realizing another
tattoo parlor has gone out of business

A teen's first-ever paycheck from a first-ever job

Hearing your loathsome ex-boss
has been arrested for a DUI

Hear Ye Roar

It's National Women's History Month and to me the surprising thing is that it takes an entire month to celebrate it. I thought we could get the whole thing out of the way in maybe an hour or so.

If I were in charge I'd have a big gathering where we'd honor all the incredible women who have made such a lasting impact on us and our world. I'd run through the list of heroines, which of course would include Joan of Arc, Pocahontas, Jane Austen, Paris Hilton, Amelia Earhart, Betty Crocker, Boy George, Virginia Wolf, Sacajawea, Miss Marple, Sasquatch, Snooki, Susan B. Anthony, June Cleaver and Aunt Jemima. (I apologize if I missed anyone.)

Next, we'd have a slideshow highlighting all their mighty achievements, and a few heartfelt words about their strength and courage and vision, followed by a big round of applause. Or a bunch of crying.

Now out to the lobby for some beers and then we'd all be home in time for the ballgame on ESPN. But seriously: a month? Oh, I know. My program for honoring those in the Women's Awareness Month, or whatever it's called, would only put the spotlight on them for 10 minutes or so each. But that's about six minutes more than the average college history professor devotes to Thomas Jefferson or Michelangelo or Thomas Edison or the Wright Brothers or Babe Ruth or George Washington

Carver or Ulysses Grant.

Folks, this whole Women's Whoopteedoo is really just a mush-up of propaganda, baloney and silliness. For the past 35 years we've been forced to listen to well-off white women blubber and grumble that for too long their great accomplishments have been ignored, their voices unheard, their history unwritten, their self-esteem unrecognized. We have failed to address their issues and concerns. We have refused to listen to their demands. We haven't read their poetry.

Yes, it's a cold, cold universe for the world's wealthiest women, and only now, in the month of March, in the year 2010, are they coming together right here in Ukiah to rise up and speak up and sing out and let the planet know of their pain and their plight.

It's utter lunacy of course, and no one but a complete fool or a member of the National Organization of Women would believe any of it. It's all just more and more complaints from the same people who've been complaining ever since 1975 when they went off to college (paid for by their dads) where they were taught to be angry and confrontational and self-righteous.

College is also where they learned to invent enemies, and all of them were men and most of the men were their fathers and uncles. Later the angry women invented their own subject matter, called women's studies, which caters to all the females on campus who believe they are big fat victims, and diseases such as bulimia, which affects about 12 women a year, all in Beverly Hills.

Next they devised a system to exclude most women from membership in their We-Are-All-Victims Club, because although Sisterhood Was Powerful, only certain women were permitted to be sisters. All others were deemed unworthy of admission into the exalted ranks of the National Organization for the Wimyns.

And the NOWsters are exactly who will be present at the Women's Time of the Month gatherings in Mendocino County, where they will gather to rejoice and celebrate and whine and weep. They won't invite local pioneers like Colleen Henderson or Marge Boynton or Martha Barra to their gathering but you can bet that every last therapist and social worker and third rate poet in the county will be milling about, exchanging hugs and sobs and support.

When it's all over they'll put out press releases telling us about their courage and commitment and community spirit. They'll tell us all about the meaningless awards they gave each other, and then they'll promise to continue their valuable work and carry on their heroic struggles until the day every bank president is a woman, and every woman is superior to any man.

Their bleatings sure do grow tiresome though, don't they? Their complaints never vary. To them the world is forever a place of raging intolerance and unfairness.

To them, no matter the changes and progress, our country is forever seething with hatred and bias and discrimination. It is forever unfair and intolerant. Forever the struggle!

To the fierce advocates of Women's History Month, it is Forever 1975.

Awards of Dubious Distinction (Cont'd)

Happiest kid in juvenile hall

Fastest runner, Ukiah Wildcat offensive line

Best cook, Ukiah high cafeteria

The real money pit:
Schools, schools, schools

The new school year has started, so try to guess how long it will take before some local member of the education aristocracy starts complaining that the schools don't have enough money.

You know it's coming. These people can't help themselves. No matter how much money the schools have—and sometimes they have a lot, and other times they have a real, *real* lot—it's never enough.

It doesn't matter how much we give to the schools because it can never be enough. No matter how many federal programs we fund, no matter how many school bond issues we pass, no matter how many local school districts we support, it isn't enough. It's not even close. Just ask a teacher. And then get ready to listen to half an hour of pitiful moaning about all the money the schools don't have.

Because the schools always need more money, regardless of how much they have. It may be a mathematical impossibility to give as much money to schools as the schools supposedly need. They need more money for programs and more money for teachers and more for books and pencils and art supplies and more to go to seminars at fancy resorts. Oops. Not really. Just kidding about the resorts. The money is really for foreign language classes, honest.

What do you think? When you hear the constant squawking from educators that there simply isn't enough money to fund the schools do you feel guilty? Do you think to yourself "Oh my, if only the taxpayers weren't such a cruel and stingy bunch of selfish pigs! If only we had voted to provide sufficient funding for school needs! After all, children are our future!"

Perhaps you fret because you didn't go to the Pomolita Bake sale last February, and worry because schools have no money to heat all those classrooms with their broken windows and leaky roofs.

Well, don't worry. Don't fret. Those would be wasted emotions, and they would go right down the drain with all the wasted money we already squander on our bloated schools.

Consider this AP story, which was printed in the Ukiah Daily Journal less than two weeks ago: "Classroom Spending Dips as Education Funding Rises" and offers details from a Pepperdine University study which showed school funding in California went from $45.6 billion in 2006 to $55.6 billion in 2009. That's a huge increase (but not enough, of course). The punchline? Spending on teachers and students actually dropped. We spent a lot more money for schools, and a lot less money went to classrooms.

I personally don't know anyone who would be even mildly surprised at such news. The study says increases in spending went primarily to "administrators and supervisors, staff travel and conferences." Sounds about right.

I have friends who work as teachers and who just returned from a weekend jaunt at some snazzy hotel in order to, I guess, learn how to teach. Been doing it 25 years, but here they go, off to some big seminar to learn even more, you betcha!

Can you think of another profession that does this? The reality is that people who actually work for a living haven't yet rigged the system to get someone else to pay for them to hang out at expensive hotels in Key West. But of course teachers are learning while they're there. I'm sure we all agree that teachers learn a whole bunch at seminars like "Strategies for Tomorrow!" and "Transformational Transitions in Education."

This is budget squander on a grand local, statewide and national scale, but right here in Ukiah the local educators rub our noses in an extra dose of sewage. At the moment the school bosses are reviewing potential building sites suitable for their lavish new office needs. This means no abandoned school or old county building will do. It's got to be something on which tens of millions of dollars can be spent, and believe me, tens of millions of dollars will be spent. You watch. The word "economize" isn't in our school district vocabulary.

Money is really never a problem for schools. There are piles of money to throw at anything from more travel on silly seminars, to extra classes for dopers and pregnant losers and violent punks. Huge new school offices are coming our way. Schools out of money? I laugh.

And yet I don't envy teachers one bit. They can have all their free seminars in Orlando and Palm Springs, and they can have their three months vacation every year. None of this makes up for the fact they have to work for the incompetent morons who run school districts. And there is certainly no solace for them in the classroom

At this point the entire profession is as dismal a career track as any that a young person might consider. A teachers' job today requires equal parts idealism and drill sergeant. I look at a roomful of teachers and all I see is a discouraged mob with the collective intelligence, hearts and courage of cattle.

Schoolteacher, thy name is Despair!

Life's Simple Pleasures (Cont'd)

Paint-by-Numbers artworks

Screaming hot spicy chili braced by
a fridge full of cold beer

Over the rainbow, two lives at a time

SCENE: Semi-dilapidated living room with maybe a couch or an over-stuffed chair, maybe a coffee table, and a television set.

STAGE IS DARK. Phone rings and after one or two rings is picked up

STAGE LIGHTENS

PETE: 'Ello? Yeah, hey Billyboy, what up? (Pause) Yeah your Giants are doing great—what next? Only way they can get rid of Zito is to eat him. A's are gonna sweep 'em this weekend. (Pause) Oh, I know—I hate that interleague stuff too. So talk, Mister Bill. (Pause) Oh no man. Really? (Pause) Evicted? You been there like eight years and they can just evict you? (Pause) Well, yeah, come down here, most definitely. Crystal moved out a month ago and she ain't coming back. There's two empty bedrooms, so move on in. (Pause) No, no, this weekend's fine. And I got my buddy in Willits—Kip, he's got a truck and he owes me one. Great. Done. See you Saturday morning. Breakfast at the truck stop. You buy.

FADE TO DARK

Lights come back on. Pete and Bill are sitting in the room, watching a ballgame.

PETE: Man oh man why do they let this guy pitch? He shouldn't even be allowed into the park without buying a ticket.

BILL: Yeah, he oughta be selling hotdogs. If I'm Billy Beane this guy's in Tacoma. (Pause) So, hey—what'd the doctor say today? You had an appointment, right?

PETE: Oh. Right. Bleeeaaah. Wants to do the surgery. Says I'll be crippled if I don't

BILL: At which point you could pitch for the Oakland A's.

PETE: Yeah but the thing is, how am I supposed to come up with money for knee surgery?

BILL: Funny.

PETE: (Pause) Huh?

BILL: Well, yeah, funny. I mean, with my paycheck the other day they had this little flyer that says there's this "significant other" benefit thing, like for a domestic partner or whatever. Somebody not your wife but still gets medical benefits. Like insurance. You know?

PETE: Like gay stuff?

BILL: No, no. Well, I mean yeah. I mean no. I mean I guess so, but it never says that. It just says you can add someone to your insurance and they're covered too. Gotta pay a little extra, but then they get medical. (Pause) I'm just saying…

FADE TO DARK

SCENE: Same room. Winter (guys maybe wearing sweatshirts)

PETE (Watching TV) Unbelievable. I can kick a football straighter than he can throw one. Wide open. Unbelievable.

BILL: Yeah, he's terrible. If they ever blow up Candlestick Park that guy oughta be strapped to the goal post. (Pause) So how's the knee doing?

PETE: Ahhh, I'm OK. Hurts, but that's what Vicodin's for. Want one?

BILL: One? Gimme a dozen. That way I can call in sick tomorrow. Maybe all week.

PETE: Doc says it looks good. X-rays next week. I'll be playing for the Warriors in a month.

BILL: Probably true, given how the Warriors look. So whadda we got here? Minute to go in the first half, Niners are down by 16. (Pause) I'm so screwed here. The A's and Giants suck, the Warriors won't win a game all next season, the Niners are a joke and I owe IRS $3700!! I'm gonna go in the kitchen and put my head in the oven.

PETE: Oven's electric.

BILL: So I'll stick my feet in a bucket of water first.

PETE: IRS?

BILL: Oh those bastards. Carol gets the home exemption thing, she gets all the deductions, gets to get credit for the kids, whatever, and I have to pay child support and now I owe the IRS $3700. Plus she's got the house and the car. Where's the bucket? Turn on the oven.

PETE (Pause) Only way it works is if you're married. Whole friggin' thing is rigged, tax-wise. Single guy gets hosed every time. In the news all the time—getting married reduces your taxes by like 60% or so. Rigged, I tell ya. (Pause) What's this? The Niners are down by 13 points and a field goal is the answer?? I need a new team.

BILL: I need a new life.

(LONG-ISH PAUSE)

PETE: See what Arnold did? Him and the Democrats worked out some deal where gay marriage is legal?

BILL: Schwarznegger did that? Gays can get married?

PETE: Said so on the news. All these legal benefits they get now. Can inherit stuff from each other, sue each other for child support, you know, the tax benefits and all....

BILL: (Pause) Tax benefits?

(Pause) Both guys slowly turn, look at each other as STAGE GOES DARK

(STAGE LIGHTENS)

It's summer. Guys wearing t-shirts, etc.

PETE: Don't pitch to this guy. Just walk him. I'd rather they got a man on first and second than pitch to Hafner here. Hafner's been killing us. Oh please walk him. Do NOT pitch to Hafner with the score tied and a man on.

BILL: The baseball gods are perverse. They hear us. They laugh in our face and proceed to do that which brings us pain. See? Knew it. They're gonna pitch to him which means

(OFFSTAGE KNOCKING ON DOOR)

PETE, (eyes remaining on TV, rises slowly and edges over to answer door)

Mumbled voices, semi-coherent exchanges/introductions and Pete re-emerges with two women of approximate same age and Bill and Pete.

PETE: So yeah, right, come on in. Great. Yeah. So this is Bill, and this is umm, Teri, and ummm?

WENDY: Wendy. Hi, nice to meet you Bill.

TERI: Hi.

BILL: Right. How ya doin'? We're just sittin here watching the A's commit suicide to Cleveland. You ladies wanna watch? Take a chair (motions vaguely). Wanna beer?

TERI: I'm a major A's fan, yeah. When they gonna get somebody to play first base?

PETE: Beer anybody? Got some Pabst Blue Ribbon, coupla Rolling Rocks....

WENDY: Great, thanks, but umm, what we came for first of all was for about three minutes-worth of help with something, and then a beer would be great.

BILL: Help?

WENDY: We're moving in across the way, over there (points) in Space 28. Anyway, I have this bookcase that's gotta be dragged out of a pickup and into the new place. You guys know Rachell— has the green Mustang, Space 19?—she told us a couple guys were living here and that maybe we could impose on you for a little help. Three minutes, tops.

(STAGE FADES TO DARK)

(Laughter and cheerful banter as the lights slowly come back on. The foursome enters the living room from offstage)

BILL: Who wants another? Whooaa—almost midnight. Man, if I call in sick tomorrow the boss will set fire to my desk.
TERI: So call in dead.
WENDY: That was fun. Great. I did not KNOW the Forest Club got so wild. You guys are great. I'm glad we moved here. We almost rented a place on South Dora…
TERI: Yeah, that was fun. We should get together again. (Pause) So…..you guys single?
Bill and Pete freeze, turn slowly and look at one another

(STAGE FADES TO DARK)

The End

She should be driving a garbage truck

When I was a kid I remember spending a fair amount of time in the summer washing cars. Not professionally, of course, just washing my parents' cars out in the driveway with a hose and a bucketful of sudsy stuff.

Keeping your car clean was passed along as a rather important thing, something that grownups did as a matter of course. I can recall using a Q-tip to polish and de-smudge the chrome fittings and trim on the dashboard of my dad's Falcon Futura, and polishing the baby moon hubcaps on the '49 Jeepster.

We assume people share our values and beliefs, and that things that are important to us are important to them. This is not always so.

When it comes to keeping her car clean my wife does not at all share my values or beliefs. While I was taught that keeping one's car tidy and bright and shiny reflected well on one's character, I do not think these lessons were passed along to Teri. I think her parents must have led her to believe that cleaning a car is not only optional, but something best left for other people to do. I am her other people. Shall we say it places a *strain* upon our relations? We shall.

I drive a fairly nice five year old car that I make some effort to keep looking reasonably spiff. I have a modest array of some necessary car products in the garage: Armor-All, wheel cleaner, some Turtle Wax. My wife wouldn't know Armor-All from Geritol. She would have no more idea of what to do with a can of car wax than with a can of Spam.

My car looks pretty good. Teri's car looks like a dumpster with a steering wheel. I try to keep her car looking tidy but she sets a brisk pace in the opposite direction. Her car is a perpetually cluttered and messy mess.

I guess I could quit my job and devote 40 hours a week to cleaning her car, but I'm not sure 40 hours a week would be enough. She can be terribly industrious.

Last week I went out to her car and took inventory. The car's back seat looked as if it didn't have one. To find it I had to burrow down through layers of newspapers, candy wrappers, towels and dog hair.

And the front seat was no better. There were beer bottles under the driver's side (*I sometimes borrow her car*). There was so much rubbish beneath the passenger side seat that I finally figured out why it no longer moves back and forth.

The glove compartment appears to be home to a family of squirrels. There are wrinkly tissues and grubby napkins lying on top of misfolded maps along with empty cigarette packs, various paperbacks stuffed in sideways and who knows what else? Probably somewhere in there is her DMV registration and proof of insurance.

Her glove compartment doubles as a pantry. You can always root around in there and come up with a few cellophane-wrapped, half-eaten granola bars, some gooey, melted chocolaty sludge that used to be inside a candy bar wrapper, but that wrapper is now in the back seat of her car, like I said a couple paragraphs ago.

There is always, 100% of the time, an opened (but uneaten) box of Animal Cracker cookies in her car. Teri nurses Animal Crackers along for months in their open box until they have gone soft and stale, which is the only way she'll eat them. I don't know. Ask a psychiatrist.

It's not just keeping her car clean that she pays no attention to. If she had a flat tire she'd drive 500 miles on the rim before she'd think to pull over. If someone suggested she check her oil she'd be genuinely puzzled. Check oil where? With what? Where's Tommy?

By process of elimination she'd eventually get to the words "engine compartment" or "under the hood" but only after she'd eliminated the trunk, because "trunk" is where she keeps all the stuff she intends to throw away that hasn't yet gone to the garage. Look under the hood? Teri has spent more time in the last 20 years looking under the refrigerator.

So I doubt I'll be getting help anytime soon with either cleaning or maintaining her automobile. She spends so much time fiddling with her makeup every morning that she can't afford to invest any in checking tire pressure or fluid levels or polishing hubcaps.

Which is fine. I probably wouldn't marry a car mechanic or a car wash attendant anyway.

Awards of Dubious Distinction (Cont'd)

Teacher of the Year,
Ukiah Unified School District

Educator of the Year,
Mendocino County Office of Education

Socrates Award, Mendocino College

Nightmare March of
The Sugar Plum Fairy

The last thing I want to do over the holidays this year is go see The Nutcracker. Let me make it 100% clear: As the 2010 Christmas season washes down the drain, the very last thing I want to sit through is The Nutcracker.

I'll explain. I've seen The Nutcracker about eight hundred times. That should be enough for any man's life. Or six lives. At this point just listening to the opening notes of "The Christmas Tree" is enough to make me cringe. Put "Spanish Dance" on and I will leave the room, and I don't care if the room is Carnegie Hall.

'Twas not always thus. There was a time I went willingly—nay, cheerfully—to see The Nutcracker. You see, in the beginning I thought taking my young daughter to The Nutcracker would be a swell treat, a pleasant holiday excursion. And so it was that in December, 1983 we went to our first-ever Nutcracker at the Ukiah High Cafetorium.

I was bored in ten minutes, and at intermission I simply told my daughter the show was over and we left. That was the last break The Nutcracker ever gave me.

By Christmas of 1984 Emily had grown more shrewd in the ways of the world (and of her father) and was taking none of my it's-over-at-intermission guff. So I squirmed and slept and checked my watch throughout the next couple Nutcrackers.

In the summer I signed Emily up for classes at The Mendocino Ballet Company. This was one of the biggest mistakes of my parenting years because her joining the ballet meant she was also joining the cast of The Nutcracker.

Which meant enduring hours and days and weeks of practice while the music of The Nutcracker played on and on and on and on and on. And every night I waited for my darling daughter to complete her two minutes of actual on-stage rehearsal time so we could get the heck out of the studio. I did this for about six weeks, clouds of Nutcracker music surrounding me at all times. Then there were approximately an infinite number of performances, and I went to every one of them. Think about that.

By 1988 I was *so very done* with The Nutcracker. But Emily wasn't. By now she'd been promoted from her early roles as a partygoer and a mouse to that of a wooden soldier, and I could hardly disrupt her flowering career as a ballerina. Who could tell? Maybe (sigh) she'd star as Clara by 1994.

But the idea I'd still be sitting through endless rehearsals and more seasons of Nutcracker torture was unthinkable. The shows and the sounds and the performances never changed. I felt trapped in a Groundhog world where "Snowflake Waltz" just keeps playing forever. By the time 1989's Nutcracker ended I had aged an extra 20 years.

And so it went. More years came and went, and so did more and more and more Nutcracker ordeals. As the holidays wore on I took to drinking before Nutcracker performances, and also out in the parking lot during intermissions. I thought if I heard "Dance of the Sugar Plum Fairy" one more time I would weep, and not from joy.

And then one year it was over. Emily's interest in ballet waned. She became involved in other things, some of which made me wonder if her being a Wooden Soldier had been such a bad idea after all.

Me? I no longer dreaded that aspect of the holidays. The twitching in my hands and shoulders stopped. The nightmares subsided. All I had to do was avoid entering stores where Nutcracker music was playing. Life was good.

But ahh, my friends, life's lessons are not for us to determine. Our fates are not in our hands. Also, the gods must be crazy. In the summer of 1994 I met my future bride, although if I'd known she had an interest in ballet she wouldn't have been. Yet it was so.

And as the winter of 1995 approached I grew wary, then terrified. It was like watching some horror movie where this sick and twisted plot traps and destroys a man. Well, actually it was more like my wife joined The Nutcracker ballet and I found myself once again attending performances and pretending to enjoy them. Love? Ha!

I think it was the following year I took up drinking in the parking lot again. By 1998 Teri had talked our neighbors, Kevin and Danna, into joining her jolly troupe of stage performers. They would visit our home and laugh and dance and listen to Nutcracker songs. In my home. Nutcracker music now played *in my home* during most evenings. How did this surreal twist happen?

I wasn't around much. I now think of the late '90s holiday seasons as The Forest Club Years.

By then I was a beaten man. A new ballet director took over the company but it changed nothing. I was drinking in the men's room during performances. I had aged. Plans were announced to do additional performances of The Nutcracker in Fort Bragg. I aged a lot more.

Then my wife got injured and could no longer perform in the ballet. Despite the temptation I wisely refrained from applauding, slapping her on the back and congratulating her because her dance career with The Nutcracker was now over. But it ended my association with the Nutcracker too. I haven't seen once since and I never will.

It's true: Our fates are not in our hands. The gods are indeed crazy, but I think they have a sense of humor.

From helping hands to helping themselves

You can't read the Ukiah Daily Journal for more than a few days and not see a bunch of stories about local organizations doing nice things for worthy causes. I see these kinds of articles all the time and in almost every instance the people doing the nice things are older folks who are members of antiquated organizations.

There's just no end to the good deeds being done around here by groups with quaint names like Elks and Moose and Masons and Soroptimists and Rotary and Lions. They pitch in every chance they get to help kids with scholarships or help build a new playground or arrange for medical services for someone in need.

Most of these organizations go back a long, long time. I would guess that here in Ukiah their membership is composed almost exclusively of older folks. Maybe the average age is 70 or so. These are our neighbors who go about the quiet work of helping others without any need to call attention to themselves as individuals.

Self promotion isn't the point. There might indeed be a story in the newspaper about how the Rotary Club is donating some new benches for a park, or how the Lions Club is going to help fix up the old Rocket Ship at Todd Grove Park, but rarely will you find anyone jumping up to take credit.

That's typical from the older generation that volunteers. These are the same folks who have sacrificed for their country and their community and their family so that the world they leave behind will be a better one.

Contrast their motives and behavior with that of the follow-up generation right here in Ukiah or all across the country. Members of the '60s generation have never given up anything unless they were getting paid for it, and preferably in advance. It's a generation that has taken far, far more than it has given and it ain't done yet.

In the early years the baby boomers took foodstamps and free college tuition and unemployment benefits. This wasn't enough. Not even close. The world was put on notice that the new generation was insufficiently pleased with what they'd been given. It demanded more.

So they staged demonstrations and riots and broke windows and burned down cities. They said they were doing it for "peace."

I'm a former hippie and I well remember when we were bursting with (imaginary) idealism, most of which was focused on the supposed hypocrisies of our parents' generation. We had a self-righteous and smug attitude, convinced we were the finest and most highly evolved people to have ever walked the planet. It was all just a monstrous load of egotistical twattle, of course, but we believed it as sure as we believed we were in the Age of Aquarius.

Those were the early days. The Love Generation next looked around and realized it now needed a way to make money off the Establishment while (a) not having to work and (b) maintaining a rebellious lifestyle.

The answer? Grants. Grants make free money available for nebulous programs with catchy titles to provide useless services for undeserving clients. So they solicited money from people who had too much of it to care where it went (governments, foundations) and began extracting cash in massive amounts.

Presto! Let a million programs bloom!

Look around Ukiah (or the country) all you want for as long as you want and you won't be able to find a single baby boomer contributing a single thing unless he's on the payroll. If someone in Ukiah is organizing any kind of local event, from a concert to a 5K run, he'll make darn sure his photo is on the front page accompanied by a lengthy biography of all the fabulous things he's done for this town.

And never forget all the proud do-gooders running things like Plow-shares and the Food Bank and the Ukiah Community Center and Project Sanctuary and the Ford Street Project and First Five, and every single one of them gets paid quite handsomely. They'll talk first and foremost, of course, about how much they care and contribute and if you want to believe it go right ahead.

County government is overstuffed with ex-hippies on its payroll, the people who spent the first half of their lives accusing others of selling out, and the second half of their lives cashing in. Every one of these people came to Ukiah from somewhere else, elbowed out the locals and burrowed in like parasites. Which they are.

You'll find mobs of them in every "community service" organization and at every one of the local nonprofits groups where they infest the boards of directors so they can hire each other and each others' spouses to squat right down in the trough of public service. It's all a nice, merry inside job and you, dear reader, are not invited. Your job is to pay the bills.

So don't look for any of these people to be on hand if there's actual work to be done because nobody from North Coast Opportunities or the Community Development Commission or SEIU is going to show up. Little League isn't their bag, man, and they don't dig the Pop Warner scene. If there's a volunteer group getting together next weekend to fix up the BMX track don't wait for a social worker or anyone from AODP to show up.

Those people will all be at the Farmer's Market where they'll be talking (and talking and talking and talking) about their "commitment to community" and their passion for the arts and their latest insights into the real estate market.

Change I can believe in

I sit 40 hours a week chained to a desk, captive of The Establishment, errand boy for The Man. In return I get enough money to pay my taxes and I don't have to sleep under a bridge.

At some point in the future I'll either get a pension or else I'll die, and I hardly care which comes first.

We all make mistakes. We can all look back with despair and regret at the choices we've made, the paths we've followed, the options we've chosen. We sit alone and ponder a muted future filled with an endless series of weeks and months and years spent at a small desk in a dim cubicle in a large office in a crummy town.

I am nearly finished with my soul-deadening "career" and a life that has all the joy and challenge of an evening of cable TV and a cold can of Spam, which is exactly what I'll be watching and eating tonight. I feel my pain.

Who knew? When I was young I had bold plans for a bright future and the unswerving determination to shape my destiny. I was going to seize the day, conquer the world and make it mine.

Where did it all go sour? Why did I give up? When did I surrender? Probably in college where I was brainwashed into thinking I was too good for the blue collar life and that I should instead focus on some sort of "professional" career. And truth be told, for a fair amount of time it worked for me. I wore a tie, I carried a briefcase and I lived the lie.

Now I want to howl. I want to throw off this yoke. I want to cast aside all that oppresses me. I want to rekindle the old spirit. I want to be who I was meant to be, and do what I was meant to do.

I believe I was meant to drive a beer truck.

Is it too late? Can I wake up tomorrow and hit the open road in my 18-wheeler, the wind in my hair, the CB radio at my side, knowing 600 Hell's Angels are counting on me to get 85 kegs of Old Milwaukee to Covelo by 8 a.m.? Count on me, lads! By the ghost of Joseph Schlitz I'll get that beer delivered on time!

I've got a lot of years to make up for. I've got a lot of living and driving to do.

If you don't hear from me don't give it a second thought. You'll never miss me because I'll never leave you.

+ When you pop the top from a Pabst Blue Ribbon, that's me.
+ When you climb up onto the bar stool and order a draft, look into the mirror and I'll be at your side.
+ When you're in an alley tossing up everything between your tonsils and your toenails I'll be with you.
+ When you're in a two-bit bar in Boonville without a buck for a beer, just roll the dice with the barkeep for a round. That's me bringing those snakeyes to life and that cold pitcher of Coors to the rescue.
+ When you have a blinding hangover I'll be there to bring you comfort and an aspirin and another frosty Mickey's Big Mouth to help you back on your feet.
+ And when you're parched and homeless and broke, I'll be the breeze in the trees that lifts a $20 bill your way, just half a block from the liquor store. Go on inside—I've left a case of Meister-brau in there with your name on it.

I've lost a lot of years sitting at a desk counting paperclips and staring at a clock. Now turn me loose on the highway of freedom and let me be that beacon of hope, that light in the wilderness, that flowing stream of ice-cold beer that leads to the empty swimming pool in your back yard.

Remember, there ain't no mountain too steep for this truck drivin' beer haulin' brother of yours. There's no town too remote that I can't find it and deliver those 12-ounce doses of refreshing medicine.

So go on ahead, and don't wait for me. Have faith that I'll find you. I'll be there.

Goodbye dear readers, and lift a mug for me!

Life's Simple Pleasures (Cont'd)

A birthday card—again this year!
—from Paris Hilton

When it dawns on you that you've never, ever seen a Monday Night Football game

Driving out of Lake County: Always a joy

. . . .

His eye was on the sparrow

I'm at a memorial service in New York today to say goodbye to my younger brother who died last week. I'm sure to be joined by the million or so friends he'd collected over the past half-century, and I know he'd have loved to be here under profoundly different circumstances.

Nobody ever made, or kept, friends like Peter Hine did. Pete might meet someone at a party or at a train station and you'd realize, 30 years later, that they were still swapping birthday cards and Christmas greetings, and that every decade or so they'd have lunch when Pete would call because he'd be stopping in Joplin later that day to change trains.

He was a wonderful friend to a lot of people. He was also the finest person I've ever known, and I've known Teri Capriolo, Dick Shoemaker, Dan Hibshman and Kip. Pete was the greatest.

I don't think I've ever been in a room, no matter how big and no matter how crowded, that Peter wouldn't have been the best person in it. I never heard a bad word said about him in my entire life and if I had I would have assumed they were talking about some other guy named Peter Hine.

No one ever had a better brother, and I will trail him to the grave wishing I'd been as good to him as he was to me. It would have been impossible. I was no match.

We grew up in Cleveland, but Cleveland has a way of scattering its young, and he wound up in New York. With my luck I drew the California card. The real winner was New York City, as it got the finest unofficial ambassador that town has ever known. Pete loved everything about New York: the people, the parks, the shops and the streets. He loved living high above the Vasmay Lounge, a 1920s-era Puerto Rican bar in SoHo. He loved railroads and family, his teenage sons (Casey and Nick) and his sister Carol, the best and truest friend he had in this world.

And he loved his job. Luck and fate crossed paths 20 years ago and resulted in Peter taking a job with the Metropolitan Transit Authority. It was a perfect match—like Babe Ruth finding work with the Yankees. He was in the real estate division, a position that allowed him to exploit his knowledge of, and love for, the city. He knew every block and building in New York, and most of its nooks and crannies and alleys and pigeons.

Pete knew where Mayor Fiorello LaGuardia had gone every Thursday to have lunch. He knew why the MTA had a subway station under the Waldorf-Astoria Hotel. He knew why the poles holding up the awnings on an apartment on Riverside Drive were made of copper on three sides and stainless steel on the fourth.

Pete knew the Chelsea Hotel had once been the tallest building in Manhattan, and which rooms in it our literary heroes had occupied. He also knew the ideal Chinese restaurant for visitors, because a certain one had a chicken in the back room that would play tic-tac-toe against you for 25 cents a game. It won every time, to Pete's delight. Lousy bird must've taken three bucks from me over the years.

And Peter was so nice. So kind. He was helpful and considerate and generous and friendly. How many times did I watch him grab the front end of a baby stroller to help a mom get it down the stairs? How many times did I see him pick litter up off the sidewalk and take it to a trash can on the next corner? There was a front page picture of him in the New York Times showing him 10 feet off the ground clutching a utility pole on Sixth Avenue while putting a baby sparrow back in its nest. If you needed a buck Peter would give you his wallet.

Years ago he worked relentlessly to help a Sri Lankan family through problems involving its subway station shop being relocated. It went on a long time, and trust me, it got complicated. The MTA had accountants, security officers and lawyers on its side, and the only thing the Sri Lanka family had was Peter. It was a fair fight.

When he was destroyed last December by a catastrophic stroke Pete lay in a coma in a hospital bed 35 miles from New York City. His regular visitors were his sister and the family from Sri Lanka who came several times weekly to pray and weep. One time the father took Carol aside to ask if Peter had been a religious man.

"No," she said. "Not really. We just weren't raised that way."

Mr. Selvaratnum accepted the news quietly, and after a while he took her hand in his own.

"It is alright," he said finally. "Okay. Because Peter, you know, he walks like Jesus."

Peter John Hine
April 4, 1953 - March 8, 2012

· · · · · · · · · · · ·

About the Author

Tom Hine grew up in Cleveland, and wound up in Ukiah as a result of "one mistake after another." He has been writing under the Tommy Wayne Kramer byline since the earliest '80s.

He works as a criminal defense investigator and in the past quarter-century has investigated scores of homicides, hundreds of assaults, countless DUIs and one matter involving animal cruelty. The victim in that case was a chicken.

He lives with his wife, Teri Capriolo.

Made in the USA
Charleston, SC
01 March 2013